THE PASSION TRANSLATION

THE PASSIONATE LIFE BIBLE STUDY SERIES

12-LESSON STUDY GUIDE

THE BOOKS OF

1&2 PETER AND JUDE

TRIUMPHANT TO THE END

BroadStreet PUBLISHING

BroadStreet Publishing® Group, LLC
Savage, Minnesota, USA
BroadStreetPublishing.com

TPT: The Books of 1 and 2 Peter and Jude: 12-Lesson Bible Study Guide

9781424570720 (softcover)
9781424570737 (ebook)

General editor: Brian Simmons
Managing editor: William D. Watkins
Writer: Andrew P. Kauth

Cover and interior by Garborg Design Works | garborgdesign.com

Printed in China

26 27 28 29 30 5 4 3 2 1

Contents

From God's Heart to Yours

"God is love," says the apostle John, and "Everyone who loves is fathered by God and experiences an intimate knowledge of him" (1 John 4:7). The life of a Christ-follower is, at its core, a life of love—God's love of us, our love of him, and our love of others and ourselves because of God's love for us.

And this divine love is reliable, trustworthy, unconditional, other-centered, majestic, forgiving, redemptive, patient, kind, and more precious than anything else we can ever receive or give. It characterizes each person of the Trinity—Father, Son, and Holy Spirit—and so is as limitless as they are. They love one another with this eternal love, and they reach beyond themselves to us, created in their image with this love.

How do we know such incredible truths? Through the primary source of all else we know about the one God—his Word, the Bible. Of course, God reveals who he is through other sources as well, such as the natural world, miracles, our inner life, our relationships (especially with him), those who minister on his behalf, and those who proclaim him to us and others. But the fullest and most comprehensive revelation we have of God and from him is what he has given us in the thirty-nine books of the Hebrew Scriptures (the Old Testament) and the twenty-seven books of the Christian Scriptures (the New Testament). Together, these sixty-six books present a compelling and telling portrait of God and his dealings with us.

It is these Scriptures that *The Passionate Life Bible Study Series* is all about. Through these study guides, we—the editors and writers of this series—seek to provide you with a unique and welcoming opportunity to delve more deeply into God's precious Word, encountering there his loving heart for you and all the others he loves. God wants you to know him more deeply, to love him more devoutly, and to share his heart with others more frequently and freely. To accomplish this, we have based this study guide series on The Passion Translation of the Bible, which strives to "reintroduce the passion and fire of the Bible to the English reader. It doesn't merely convey the literal meaning of words. It expresses God's passion for people and his world by translating the original, life-changing message of God's Word for modern readers." It has been created to "kindle in you a burning desire to know the heart of God, while impacting the church for years to come."[1]

In each study guide, you will find an introduction to the Bible book it covers. There you will gain information about that Bible book's authorship, date of composition, first recipients, setting, purpose, central message, and key themes. Each lesson following the introduction will take a portion of that Bible book and walk you through it so you will learn its content better while experiencing and applying God's heart for your own life and encountering ways you can share his heart with others. Along the way, you will come across a number of features we have created that provide opportunities for more life application and growth in biblical understanding.

Experience God's Heart

This feature focuses questions on personal application. It will help you live out God's Word and to bring the Bible into your world in fresh, exciting, and relevant ways.

Share God's Heart

This feature will help you grow in your ability to share with other people what you learn and apply in a given lesson. It provides guidance on using the lesson to grow closer to others and to enrich your fellowship with others. It also points the way to enabling you to better listen to the stories of others so you can bridge the biblical story with their stories.

The Backstory

This feature provides ancient historical and cultural background that illuminates Bible passages and teachings. It deals with then-pertinent religious groups, communities, leaders, disputes, business trades, travel routes, customs, nations, political factions, ancient measurements and currency...in short, anything historical or cultural that will help you better understand what Scripture says and means.

Word Wealth

This feature provides definitions for and other illuminating information about key terms, names, and concepts, and how different ancient languages have influenced the biblical text. It also provides insight into the different literary forms in the Bible, such as prophecy, poetry, narrative history, parables, and letters, and how knowing the form of a text can help you better interpret and apply it. Finally, this feature highlights the most significant passages in a Bible book. You may be encouraged to memorize these verses or keep them before you in some way so you can actively hide God's Word in your heart.

Digging Deeper

This feature explains the theological significance of a text or the controversial issues that arise and mentions resources you can use to help you arrive at your own conclusions. Another way to dig deeper into the Word is by looking into the life of a biblical character or another person from church history, showing how that man or woman incarnated a biblical truth or passage. For instance, Jonathan Edwards was well known for his missions work among native American Indians and for his intellectual prowess in articulating the Christian faith, Florence Nightingale for the reforms she brought about in healthcare, Irenaeus for his fight against heresy, Billy Graham for his work in evangelism, Moses for the strength God gave him to lead the Hebrews and receive and communicate the law, and Deborah for her work as a judge in Israel. This feature introduces to you figures from the past who model what it looks like to experience God's heart and share his heart with others.

The Extra Mile

While The Passion Translation's notes are extensive, sometimes students of Scripture like to explore more on their own. In this feature, we provide you with opportunities to glean more information from a Bible dictionary, a Bible encyclopedia, a reliable Bible online tool, another ancient text, and the like. Here you will learn how you can go the extra mile on a Bible lesson. And not just in study either. Reflection, prayer, discussion, and applying a passage in new ways provide even more opportunities to go the extra mile. Here you will find questions to answer and applications to make that will require more time and energy from you—if and when you have them to give.

As you can see above, each of these features has a corresponding icon so you can quickly and easily identify them.

You will find other helps and guidance through the lessons of these study guides, including thoughtful questions, application suggestions, and spaces for you to record your own reflections, answers, and action steps. Of course, you can also write in your own journal, notebook, computer document, or other resource, but we have provided you with space for your convenience.

Also, each lesson will direct you toward the introductory material and numerous notes provided in The Passion Translation. There each Bible book contains a number of aids supplied to help you better grasp God's words and his incredible love, power, knowledge, plans, and so much more. We want you to get the most out of your Bible study, especially using it to draw you closer to the One who loves you most.

Finally, at the end of each lesson you'll find a section called "Talking It Out." This contains questions and exercises for application that you can share, answer, and apply with your spouse, a friend, a coworker, a Bible study group, or any other individuals or groups who would like to walk with you through this material. As Christians, we gather together to serve, study, worship, sing, evangelize, and a host of other activities. We grow together, not just on our own. This section will give you ample opportunities to engage others with some of the content of each lesson so you can work it out in community.

We offer all of this to support you in becoming an even more faithful and loving disciple of Jesus Christ. A disciple in the ancient world was a student of her teacher, a follower of his master. Students study, and followers follow. Jesus' disciples are to sit at his feet and listen and learn and then do what he tells them and shows them to do. We have created *The Passionate Life Bible Study Series* to help you do what a disciple of Jesus is called to do.

So go.

Read God's words.

Hear what he has to say in them and through them.

Meditate on them.

Hide them in your heart.

Display their truths in your life.

Share their truths with others.

Let them ignite Jesus' passion and light in all you say and do.

Use them to help you fulfill what Jesus called his disciples to do: "Now wherever you go, make disciples of all nations, baptizing them in the name of the Father, the Son, and the Holy Spirit. And teach them to faithfully follow all that I have commanded you. And never forget that I am with you every day, even to the completion of this age" (Matthew 28:19–20).

And through all of this, let Jesus' love nourish your heart and allow that love to overflow into your relationships with others (John 15:9–13). For it was for love that Jesus came, served, died, rose from the dead, and ascended into heaven. This love he gives us. And this love he wants us to pass along to others.

Why I Love the Letters of Peter and Jude

In a world brimming with uncertainty, persecution, and moral confusion, few portions of Scripture speak as directly and compassionately to the believer as the epistles of 1 Peter, 2 Peter, and Jude. These letters are short, yet they are saturated with divine wisdom, encouragement, and sobering truth. What makes me love these books deeply is not merely their theology or their literary beauty but the way they unveil the tender and fierce heart of God for his people living in difficult times.

1 Peter: The Shepherding Heart of God

First Peter was written to believers scattered and suffering—people who had been marginalized, oppressed, and misunderstood. Right from the start, Peter reminds them of their identity: chosen by God, sanctified by the Spirit, and sprinkled with the blood of Jesus Christ (1 Peter 1:2). In the midst of their trials, Peter does not offer shallow comfort. He doesn't tell them to escape hardship, but instead he lifts their gazes toward a living hope through the resurrection of Jesus (v. 3). This hope is not an abstract idea; it is an inheritance that is "imperishable, undefiled, and unfading, kept in heaven" (v. 4).

What I find especially moving about 1 Peter is its pastoral tone. Peter—once impulsive and brash—has become a tender shepherd, just as Jesus commanded him to be (John 21:15–17). He writes to strengthen the faith of Christians who feel like exiles, reminding them that even in their suffering, they are a holy priesthood, called to declare the excellencies of God (1 Peter 2:9). This letter reveals the heart of our divine Father who does not abandon his children in suffering but walks with them, refining their faith like gold tested by fire (1:7).

The call to holiness, submission, and love in 1 Peter is not a burden but an invitation to reflect the character of the God who is both holy and compassionate. This letter reminds me that God sees, God cares, and God strengthens. In the face of ridicule or persecution, it affirms that suffering for righteousness is not a sign of abandonment—it is a mark of fellowship with Christ.

2 Peter: God's Patience and the Call to Remain Steadfast

If 1 Peter offers comfort to the suffering, 2 Peter issues a clarion call to remain rooted in truth amid deception. I love 2 Peter because it reveals another aspect of God's heart: his patience and his unwavering commitment to truth. Peter opens the letter by reminding believers that God has given us "everything we need for life and godliness" (2 Peter 1:3). That includes not just strength to endure but also discernment to recognize what is true in a world full of lies.

One of the most powerful verses in this book is 3:9: "The Lord is not slow to fulfill his promise as some understand slowness, but is patient with you, not wanting anyone to perish, but everyone to come to repentance." Here we see a God whose delay in judgment is not apathy but mercy. In a time when scoffers questioned the return of Christ and moral decay was rampant, Peter's words provided assurance: God's justice will come, but so will his grace, extended as long as possible to a rebellious world.

What I cherish about 2 Peter is how it urges believers to grow—to supplement their faith with virtue, knowledge, self-control, and love (1:5–7). In other words, spiritual stagnation is not an option. This letter reminds me that in troubled times, faithfulness is not passive endurance but active pursuit. It gives me confidence that God equips his people not just to survive in dark days but also to shine.

Jude: Contending for the Faith with Mercy

The book of Jude, though brief, is one of the most powerful and urgent calls to spiritual vigilance in the New Testament. I love Jude because it holds together two essential truths: the fierce call to contend for the faith and the gentle mandate to show mercy. Jude begins with a stunning affirmation: believers are "called, beloved in God the Father and kept for Jesus Christ" (Jude 1). In those few words, we see the security and affection God has for his people.

Jude's tone is bold as he exposes false teachers and urges believers to stand firm. Yet, his letter never descends into anger or cynicism. Instead, it radiates the holiness of God and the compassion that comes from understanding the human struggle. "Have mercy on those who doubt," Jude says (v. 22). In a time when deception ran rampant, God still had compassion for the confused, the weak, and the wavering.

The doxology at the end of Jude may be one of the most beautiful in Scripture: "Now to him who is able to keep you from stumbling and to present you blameless before the presence of his glory with great joy" (v. 24). These words make my heart sing. They remind me that God is not only able to protect me from error and sin, but he also delights to present me before himself with joy. That is a glimpse into the very heart of God—a God who saves, sanctifies, and rejoices over his people.

Hope That Abounds

I love 1 and 2 Peter and Jude because they do not flinch in the face of hardship, heresy, or heartache. They tell the truth about suffering, deception, and spiritual warfare. But more than that, they reveal a God who shepherds his people with tenderness, equips them with power, and keeps them by his mercy. In these letters, I find hope, courage, and an unshakable assurance that in troubled times, God is near, God is working, and God is coming again.

General Editor

LESSON 1

1 Peter: Hope Is the Treasure

(1 Peter 1:1–12)

It's nearly impossible to talk about the apostle Peter, let alone begin a study of any text related to him, without recalling Jesus' specific words regarding Peter in Matthew 16. After Peter's confession of Jesus as the "Anointed One" (the Christ, or Messiah) in verse 16, Jesus gave Peter his new name and stated the importance of Peter's confession in verse 18: "I give you the name Peter, a stone. And this rock will be the bedrock foundation on which I will build my church—my legislative assembly, and the power of death will not be able to overpower it!"

Truly, Peter's confession that Jesus was the promised Messiah, "the Son of the living God" (v. 16), is the "bedrock foundation" (v. 17) for the church.[2] It was God the Father who revealed this foundational truth to Peter (v. 17). And while Peter was not without his faults, his faith was unparalleled: from immediately following Jesus when called (4:18–20), to stepping out of a boat in the midst of a storm to walk on water with Jesus (14:28–30), to preaching the gospel to thousands of Jews in Jerusalem on Pentecost (Acts 2:14–41), Peter demonstrated, time and again, not only his faith but also how much he loved Jesus. What a blessing to have his words preserved for all believers today—words that will no doubt leave your faith encouraged and strengthened!

Authorship

As stated in 1 Peter 1:1, the apostle Peter is the author of this book of the Bible, one of the New Testament's general epistles. And while Peter's authorship here is not widely doubted, there are a few scholars who question his authorship due to the classical, complex nature of the Greek used in the letter itself. They reason that because Peter was an uneducated fisherman (Matthew 4:18; Acts 4:13), he would not have been able to write as well as the Greek indicates. However, as Brian Simmons notes about 1 Peter, "Every good writer has a brilliant editor. Peter's editor for this letter was Silvanus (5:12), who no doubt helped Peter with the more elegant Greek words...which are found in these five chapters."[3] Despite the unexpected higher linguistic usage in the letter, both church tradition and the majority of modern scholars agree to the Petrine authorship of 1 Peter.[4]

The man Peter needs little introduction. Peter clearly led the apostles. Often their spokesman, he was prominently placed at the head of the various lists of apostles by the Gospel writers (Matthew 10:2–4; Mark 3:16–19; Luke 6:13–16; Acts 1:13). Originally from a family of fishermen who lived in Bethsaida and later Capernaum, Peter came to follow Jesus along with his brother, the apostle Andrew (John 1:40–42). Peter's early exploits after Jesus' resurrection and ascension are chronicled in Acts 1–12. He was empowered to take the lead as the main preacher of the gospel message on Pentecost, and he also went on to perform many notable miracles. In addition, and maybe even more significantly, he opened the door to the spreading of the gospel to both the Samaritans (Acts 8:14–17) and the gentiles (Acts 10).

THE BACKSTORY

Peter most likely wrote this letter around AD 64, when much of Rome was destroyed by fire and Christians were subsequently blamed and persecuted. Debate surrounds the origins of the fire, though, and many place the blame on the Roman emperor

Nero himself. According to the historian Suetonius (69–ca. 122), for example, Nero set fire to Rome, later blaming the Christians, because he despised the city's aesthetics and couldn't get Senate approval for his various building projects.[5] Moreover, the Roman historian and politician Tacitus (56–ca. 120) recounts,

> A disaster followed, whether accidental or treacherously contrived by the emperor, is uncertain...more dreadful than any which have ever happened to this city by the violence of fire....But all human efforts, all the lavish gifts of the emperor, and the propitiations of the gods, did not banish the sinister belief that the conflagration was the result of an order [from Nero]. Consequently, to get rid of the report, Nero fastened the guilt and inflicted the most exquisite tortures on a class hated for their abominations, called Christians by the populace. Christus, from whom the name had its origin, suffered the extreme penalty during the reign of Tiberius at the hands of one of our procurators, Pontius Pilatus, and a most mischievous superstition, thus checked for the moment, again broke out not only in Judæa, the first source of the evil, but even in Rome, where all things hideous and shameful from every part of the world find their centre and become popular. Accordingly, an arrest was first made of all who pleaded guilty; then, upon their information, an immense multitude was convicted, not so much of the crime of firing the city, as of hatred against mankind. Mockery of every sort was added to their deaths. Covered with the skins of beasts, they were torn by dogs and

> perished, or were nailed to crosses, or were doomed to the flames and burnt, to serve as a nightly illumination, when daylight had expired.[6]

Regardless of the source of the great fire of Rome, Nero's need for a scapegoat set the stage for a dangerous atmosphere for Christians living in and around the capital city at the time. In fact, it was during the last years of Nero's reign that he executed Peter and Paul.[7]

As we'll see later in our study of 1 Peter, not all persecution came by fire or sword. Peter wrote to Christians who lived in what we know today as Turkey. They were enduring "words of ridicule, slander and sometimes formal accusations of crimes against society (see 1 Pet 2:12; 3:13–17; 4:14–16)."[8] Their Roman pagan neighbors didn't understand (1) their refusal to worship the Roman emperor while displaying loyalty to a God who created all peoples, (2) their distinctive worship of one God rather than many gods, (3) their lives of virtue over those of sensuous pleasures, and (4) their commitment to one spouse rather than having concubines on the side. The Christians' differences often worked against them, and yet the apostle Peter exhorted them to maintain those differences for their sakes and for those of their pagan Roman neighbors.

- *How would you feel, as a Christian, living under a government run by a leader such as Nero?*

- *Persecution appears in many forms, not just in physical violence. What are some other forms of persecution?*

- *Do you know anyone who has faced religious persecution? (Perhaps that person is you.) If you do, recount what kind of persecution this person endured and how he or she handled it.*

Recipients of Peter's Letter

Peter specifically named his audience in the first chapter of his letter: "the chosen ones who have been scattered like 'seed' into the nations living as refugees in Pontus, Galatia, Cappadocia, and throughout the Roman provinces of Asia and Bithynia" (v. 1). Peter's initial audience was comprised of Jewish and gentile Christians who were scattered throughout Roman-controlled Asia Minor. People from this part of the Roman Empire were present when the Holy Spirit fell upon Jesus' followers in Jerusalem and caused them to speak in foreign human languages they had not learned (Acts 2:1–11). Years later, the apostle Paul preached and taught in some of the Asian provinces (18:23; 19:8–10, 26).

The Christians in these provinces were scattered due to persecution. Peter wrote to them, not realizing that his own crucifixion was only a few years away.[9] He wanted these believers to remain faithful to the Lord to the end. He also wanted to encourage them to live in such a way that they would stand against the ways of the world and live in a way that would make them truly stand out as beacons of hope and light among unbelievers. Peter wanted Christians to be fully sold out, living only for God, no matter the costs. His simple message: faithfully endure, because, as followers of Jesus, we have a triumphant hope!

- *Have you ever received an encouraging message (a letter, a phone call, an email, or even a text), especially at a time when you may have felt discouraged, hopeless, or lost? What was the situation? How did that message encourage you?*

Major Themes

Four themes dominate Peter's first epistle: (1) the nature of God; (2) the nature of salvation; (3) life in the family of God; and (4) life in the midst of suffering and persecution.

1) The Nature of God

For Peter, God is a triune God (God the Father, God the Son, and God the Holy Spirit), which is, of course, a universal truth held by all historic orthodox churches and denominations. Who God is and what God is like is of utmost importance to Peter. Peter talked of God as our Creator and as our Judge. These are actions often attributed to God the Father. Then, as our Redeemer, God the Son is, as Peter loved to call him, the "Anointed One" (1 Peter 1:7). His suffering and crucifixion assure all believers of their salvation. And God the Holy Spirit? Well, he is vital for the Christian life. He is God inside of us, the individual Christian's source of the revelation of the gospel and collective Christians' power as they live their lives, waiting for the return of Jesus.

- *Peter refers to God as "Father God" straightaway: "You are not forgotten, for you have been chosen and destined by Father God" (1:2). In what ways have you encountered God as your Father?*

- *Jesus was revealed as "the Son of the living God" while he walked on the earth. This is Peter's confession in Matthew 16:16. How will this fact be reinforced when Jesus returns to earth (Titus 2:13–14; Revelation 19:11–16; 20:4–6)?*

- *Peter stated that "the Holy Spirit has set you apart to be God's holy ones, obedient followers of Jesus Christ who have been gloriously sprinkled with his blood" (1 Peter 1:2). How has the Holy Spirit empowered you to live as a follower of Jesus, obedient and set apart? What revelations or encouragements to remain faithful have you received from the Holy Spirit?*

2) The Nature of Salvation

Peter described salvation through Jesus with different images and phrases throughout 1 Peter. In the first chapter, for example, he talked about being sprinkled with Jesus' blood (v. 2) and being redeemed through Jesus' precious blood (vv. 18–19). Moreover, chapters 2 and 3 explain how the sacrifice of Jesus has allowed Christians to experience God's goodness and kindness, bringing them closer to God.

- *How has Jesus' blood purified and changed your life?*

- *When you are born again (1:23), what are you reborn into? When were you born again? What did you inherit in that moment?*

3) Life in the Family of God

Peter did not envision the Christian life to be a life lived alone. The church, for Peter, was a united body of believers who live as a true family of God. He even went so far as referring to Christians as a "spiritual 'nation'" (2:9).

- *Read 1 Peter 1:1 and 5:14. How do the first and last verses of 1 Peter reflect the theme of Christians living as a family?*

4) Life in the Midst of Suffering and Persecution

A consequence of living as a member of the family of God—set apart from the world—is the very likely reality of being at odds with the world. And persecution, suffering, and trials go along with that. The persecution of Christians was very real at the time Peter wrote, just as it's a current reality for many Christians throughout the world today. Christians are truly called to be "resident aliens and foreigners in this world" (2:11). But there is hope, because God never fails, and heaven awaits the faithful.

- *Peter wrote several times about believers suffering: 1:6–7; 3:13–17; 4:12–19; and 5:9. Read through those passages. Peter was certain that obedience would inevitably bring about trials. What difficulties have you faced as you've lived as a Christian, especially if you've stood for Jesus in the face of direct opposition? How have such trials revealed the strength of your faith?*

Salvation and Hope

Have you ever restored a piece of furniture, stripping off all the old paint or stain, filling or patching old dings and holes, sanding it, and finally repainting it or giving it a few new coats of stain? Maybe you've completed some renovations in your current home. Or maybe you've gone all in and restored an entire house. Restoration is a lot of work. Likely, your hope of an amazing end product carried you through to the end, and the result was something truly unique and beautiful—something that became a real treasure. Hopefully, all that painstaking work was worth it—your vision came to life, and the old was made new.

In 1 Peter 1:3–9, Peter described God's mercy and how it allows for Christians to experience a true living hope through Jesus' resurrection. A Christian's faith in Jesus secures the ultimate treasure, salvation. And despite all kinds of trials, this salvation grants hope. Indeed, the hope that all Christians have in their eternal salvation is, as Peter said, a cause to "jump for joy" (v. 6).

- *Read 1 Peter 1:3–9. How does verse 4, in particular, serve as an encouragement for Peter's fellow Christians scattered throughout the Roman world? How can it serve as an encouragement for you, especially when you face potential trials?*

From the beginning, God's plan was salvation. Peter detailed in verses 10–12 how the prophets of the Old Testament embodied the spirit of Christ. Without a doubt, those prophets understood that their inspired words were meant for their generation as well as for the generations to come.

- *Read 1 Peter 1:10–12. In verse 12, Peter talked about how God's gospel for the world is something "that even the angels long to get a glimpse of." Are you amazed by the gospel—the good news of the Savior and the salvation he provides by faith? If so, what about it brings you to wonder and awe?*

EXPERIENCE GOD'S HEART

The first chapter of 1 Peter provides a lot of opportunity for reflection on how God works in our lives.

- *Read verses 5–7. Note that salvation includes three stages: salvation from sin's penalty, which is called justification; salvation from sin's power, which is called sanctification; and salvation from sin's presence, which is called glorification. So what Peter called "our full salvation" (v. 5) is the culmination of salvation—glorification, which will occur when we receive our resurrection bodies and enter into a new creation forever free of sin and its corrupting power. What does it mean that "God constantly guards us" until we are glorified? Peter made it clear that this guarding does not preclude experiencing trials and grief. So what does it involve?*

- *The goal of God's work in our lives is to refine us, to shape and strengthen our faith (v. 7). What will be the result of this?*

- *What has been your experience of God's guarding efforts in your life? How has his work impacted your faith?*

SHARE GOD'S HEART

A firm understanding of how to stay both faithful and joyful in any circumstance will definitely leave you standing strong! And your ability to remain faithful and filled with joy, regardless of what life throws at you, will also serve as an amazing testimony for others.

- *Was there a time in your life when your faith wavered in the face of difficulty? How did that affect you and those around you?*

- *Are you the kind of person who is filled with joy no matter the situation? Why or why not?*

- *Imagine what it was like for the Christians in Rome around the mid AD 60s to be driven from their homes, persecuted, and often killed. How can your response to the trials you've experienced—or possibly are even experiencing currently—serve as a testimony to your faith in God? How can that response serve as an encouragement for those around you, both believers and unbelievers alike?*

Talking It Out

Since Christians grow in community, not just in solitude, here are some questions you may want to discuss with another person or in a group. Each "Talking It Out" section is designed with this purpose in mind.

1. Peter definitely emphasized the importance of experiencing God in his triune nature. In fact, he immediately mentioned "Father God," "the Holy Spirit," and "Jesus Christ" in verse 2. Discuss your understanding of the Trinity.

2. How have you—and how do you—experience God as Father, Son, and Holy Spirit?

3. According to verse 4, a Christian's inheritance (the fullness of salvation) is guaranteed. How did Peter describe this inheritance? Does it sound like something you can count on? Why or why not?

LESSON 2

Standing Out in a Crowd

(1 Peter 1:13–2:17)

Do you like to stick out in a crowd? Or are you the type of person who likes to blend in? Were you the kid who loved to sit in front of the class? Or do you like to show up right when church starts and grab a seat in the back so you don't have to talk to a lot of people? It would be a strange world if everyone tried to stick out in a crowd or if everyone wanted to blend in. Likewise, everyone can't sit in the front, and there isn't room for everyone in the back.

In 1 Peter 1:13–25 and 2:1–17, Peter called Christians to action—action that will make them stand out in this fallen world. It's action that pursues holiness. Holiness is a very high standard. And whether you're the type of person who likes to stand out or blend in, living a life of holiness will definitely have you stand out in today's world, just as it would have in the days of the early church when Peter was living, preaching, and writing. To get ready for this pursuit, we need to follow Peter's advice and "prepare your hearts and minds for action!" (1:13).

WORD WEALTH

Before we delve into more of the details of 1 Peter, let's dig into the concept of holiness. Peter referenced Leviticus 11:44 and 19:2 in 1:16 of his letter: "For Scripture says: 'You are to be holy, because I am holy.'" Leviticus 11:44 and 19:2 say the following, respectively: "For I am the Lord your God. Consecrate yourselves therefore, and be holy, for I am holy"; "You shall be holy, for I the Lord your God am holy" (ESV).

The Hebrew word for holy used in these passages of Scripture is *qadosh*, which means "sacred" and is most often used as an adjective and translated as holy. The word is first used in Exodus 19:6, where God called his people, the Israelites, to be a "kingdom of priests and a holy nation" (ESV). A deeper dive into the Hebrew meaning revealed this:

> In the Old Testament *qadosh* has a strongly religious connotation. In one sense the word describes an object or place or day to be 'holy' with the meaning of 'devoted' or 'dedicated' to a particular purpose....God has dedicated Israel as His people. They are 'holy' by their relationship to 'holy' God.... God's intent was to use this 'holy' nation as a 'holy,' royal priesthood amongst the nations (Ex. 19:6). Based on the intimate nature of the relationship, God expected His people to live up to His 'holy' expectations and, thus, to demonstrate that they were a 'holy nation.'[10]

Holiness, then, is the high standard that Peter promoted in this section of his letter. In the Greek, the word for "holy" is *hagios*, which "fundamentally signifies separated, and hence, in Scripture in its moral and spiritual significance, separated from sin and therefore consecrated to God, sacred."[11]

- *Read TPT's footnote for 1 Peter 1:16. What does this footnote tell you about what holiness includes and what it is?*

Pursuing Holiness

For Peter, holiness was a high calling, a true mark of the Christian. It was a state of being that will necessitate believers standing apart from unbelievers.

- *For each of the following, (1) look up the verse, reading the entire passage in context; (2) define for yourself what Peter meant as he himself describes holiness; and (3) write down your thoughts about how you can better shape your life to be less like you were before you knew Jesus and more like you are now, striving "to become like the Holy One who called you" (1:15).*

1:17 — "Live each day with holy awe and reverence"

1:22 — "Be full of love for your fellow believers"

2:1 — "Abandon every form of evil, deceit, hypocrisy, feelings of jealousy and slander"

2:2 — "Crave the pure spiritual milk of God's Word"

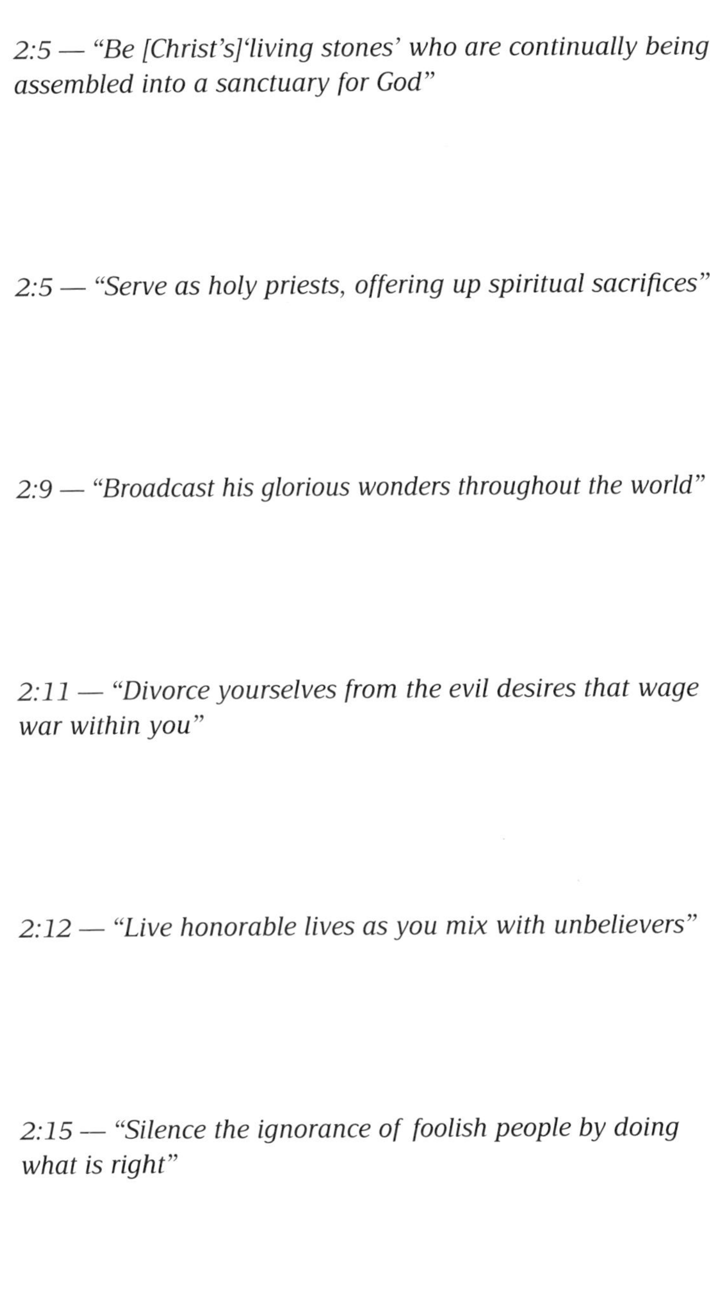

2:5 — "Be [Christ's]'living stones' who are continually being assembled into a sanctuary for God"

2:5 — "Serve as holy priests, offering up spiritual sacrifices"

2:9 — "Broadcast his glorious wonders throughout the world"

2:11 — "Divorce yourselves from the evil desires that wage war within you"

2:12 — "Live honorable lives as you mix with unbelievers"

2:15 — "Silence the ignorance of foolish people by doing what is right"

2:16 — "Never use your freedom as a cover-up for evil"

2:17 — "Recognize the value of every person....Honor your rulers"

Jesus, the Living Stone

In 2:4–8, Peter called on Christians to be "'living stones,'" referencing several Old Testament passages: Isaiah 28:16 (1 Peter 2:6); Psalm 118:22 (1 Peter 2:7); and Isaiah 8:14 (1 Peter 2:8). Peter was describing a house that God is building, a kind of spiritual house.

- *How is the church, metaphorically speaking, like a house? Do you see modern Christianity functioning in this way? If not, what are Christians missing from Peter's message here in chapter 2?*

Of course, this spiritual house of God starts with Jesus, who is *the* living stone. Certainly, Peter called Jesus a stone because of Peter's familiarity with the prophecies he quotes, and likely because Jesus referred to himself as a stone, specifically a cornerstone (Matthew 21:42, for example): "Jesus said to them, 'Haven't you ever read the Scripture that says: The very stone the builder rejected as flawed has now become the most important cornerstone. This was the Lord's plan—isn't it marvelous to behold?'" Jesus is the chief cornerstone of God's spiritual house.

- *While modern construction no longer requires the use of a cornerstone—though they are often used for ceremonial and/or decorative purposes—ancient construction relied heavily upon the cornerstone. The cornerstone set the tone for the particular building project. It was often placed first, joined the main walls, and was used to set the level, angle, and outer dimensions of the building. In what ways does Jesus serve as a cornerstone in your life? And, conversely, how might unbelievers stumble over Jesus and his message (1 Peter 2:8)?*

With Jesus as the cornerstone, believers themselves become the building blocks, living stones that, once integrated with Christ and one another, are built up and assembled together, forming God's spiritual house.

- *What is the stated purpose of God's spiritual house (2:5)?*

- *Read Psalm 118. What type of stone is Jesus? Of course, he is a living stone and a cornerstone, but as you read through Psalm 118, make a list of the attributes, characteristics, etc. of the Lord. How have you seen the Lord act in these ways in your own life?*

EXPERIENCE GOD'S HEART

- *Peter told believers to "keep coming to him [Jesus Christ] who is the Living Stone" (1 Peter 2:4). How often do you go to Jesus? How often do you turn to him in prayer and praise, or in repentance and gratitude, or in wonder and awe, or in love and obedience? You can speak to him or remain in silence before him. You can sing to him or petition him. He loves us and wants to hear from us, and spend time with us. So go to him, even now. Linger in his presence. Rest in the wonderful peace that only he can provide. Return to him over and over again. He will always receive you.*

- *God's will for us is sometimes wrapped in mystery, but more often than not, God makes it clear in his written Word what his will is for us. One of these clear expressions of his will is given in 2:15: "For it is God's will for you to silence the ignorance of foolish people by doing what is right." And what is right? What the infinite Source of goodness informs us is right. Review 1 Peter 2:1–17. Jot down at least three things that Peter, God's spokesman, told Christians to do. Each of these things is the right thing to do. Choose at least one of them to put into practice this week. And each time you do what is right, remind yourself that you are doing God's will. Be sure to call on him to help you fulfill his will in that right action. That's a prayer God delights in answering.*

- *In 2:9, Peter called Christians "God's chosen treasure," "priests who are kings," and "a spiritual 'nation' set apart as God's devoted ones." How do those descriptions help you better experience God's heart for you? And, relatedly, how do they inform your sense of identity and purpose?*

SHARE GOD'S HEART

Pursuing holiness in a world that seems to be going in the opposite direction is no joke. After all, standing out when pursuing holiness? That's easy. Staying on the narrow path of holiness? That's hard!

- *Read Matthew 7:13–14. Why do you think "nearly everyone chooses [the] crowded road!"?*

- *Have you ever found it challenging to tell others about Jesus, especially when they notice you living set apart and pursuing holiness? Have you ever experienced people being drawn to you because of how you pursue a life marked by your faith in Jesus? Write about what you have discovered and experienced.*

- *How can your daily actions better reflect God's heart in a way that is compelling and transformative to those around you? Are there any specific attitudes or behaviors that you might need to work on? In general, what type of attitude and behaviors should a Christian cultivate to better align with their calling to be "a sanctuary for God" and to "serve as holy priests" (1 Peter 2:5)?*

Talking It Out

1. How does the illustration of believers as living stones being built into a spiritual house (1 Peter 2:5) shape your understanding of your role within the church, both locally and globally? How can you support your Christian community as you are all built up in God's spiritual house? Share a few ideas or some ways in which you have experienced or seen this illustration in action.

2. How does Peter's teaching about living as free people yet not "[using] freedom as a cover-up for evil" (v. 16) inform your understanding of Christian freedom and responsibility?

3. Recall that one of the themes of 1 Peter 1 is living in the midst of trials. How can you prepare yourselves and those who are a part of your Christian community—whether immediate family, friends, or other members of your local church—to better prepare for this potential (and likely) reality? Are there any specific actions you can take in order to ensure that your pursuit of holiness will not be deterred when the world comes against you?

LESSON 3

Living Under Authority

(1 Peter 2:18–25)

Every human being has to live under the authority of another. Children live under their parents' authority. Employees have employers to answer to. Attorneys are subject to judges and their decisions as well as to the owners of their law firms. In a representative republic, such as the United States of America, politicians are ultimately responsible to their citizen constituency, for those citizens have the power to vote those political leaders out of office. Even the US president, congressional leaders, and Supreme Court justices are subject to the laws of the land. And every person who has ever lived or will live is under the Authority of all authorities, the Creator of heaven and earth, the King of kings and Lord of lords—God himself.

Recall that Peter's first readers were facing persecution under the Roman officials who had political authority over them. Christians were governed by Roman law and Roman leaders, as were all other Roman citizens and everyone else who lived in the Roman Empire. How were these Christians supposed to live their lives under pagan rule? Moreover, how were these Christians to live in work relationships where they found themselves under the authority of a pagan boss—or maybe a boss who was a self-avowed Christian but still treated employees unjustly? How were these believers supposed to handle such situations?

A Lifestyle of Holiness

Before Peter spoke about living under pagan authority, he spent time reminding his readers who they were: "chosen and destined by Father God" and set apart "to be God's holy ones" by the Holy Spirit, which would lead to them becoming "obedient followers of Jesus Christ" (1 Peter 1:2). He talked about how they were spiritually reborn "into a perfect inheritance" that would last forever (v. 4). He mentioned how their faith was being refined by the fire of trials and how that would exalt Jesus and ultimately lead to the victory of their souls (vv. 7, 9).

Then Peter called on his readers to pursue a life of holiness: "Shape your lives to become like the Holy One who called you" (v. 15). This life of holiness involves "obedience to the truth" (v. 22), "love for your fellow believers" (v. 22), abandoning "every form of evil" (2:1), craving and following God's Word (v. 2), serving as "holy priests" (v. 5), and living as "resident aliens and foreigners in this world" (v. 11). This life includes keeping ourselves "from the evil desires that wage war within you" (v. 11). And this private, personal moral choice is to be coupled with living "honorable lives as you mix with unbelievers, even though they accuse you of being evildoers" (v. 12). Peter wanted his readers to have public lives that matched their inner choice to fight against the pull of evil. Publicly and privately, Christians were to live God's way, even if unbelievers falsely accused them and treated them unjustly.

It's in this context that we must understand Peter's instruction about living under pagan authority. Even though our ultimate citizenship is heavenly, we still live in this earthly, fallen world, and we will live under the authority of others, including the authority of unbelievers. How should we then live? According to Peter, we should live as Christians set apart to be holy, to follow divine directives in our private and public lives.

- *Now, reread 1 Peter 2:13 and compare it with verse 18. Which earthly authorities are Christians supposed to submit to? Who are we supposed to honor (v. 17)?*

- *Why are we supposed to submit to pagan authorities? What will our moral actions do (v. 15)?*

- *While Peter contended that ruling authorities are supposed "to punish lawbreakers and to praise those who do what's right" (v. 14), he doesn't assume that everything those authorities actually do will be good or wise or even well-informed. What does Peter say that would apply to at least some ruling authorities (v. 15)?*

- *In contrast to how pagan authorities and even neighbors think and act, how are Christians supposed to order their lives (vv. 16–17)?*

- *Peter understood that Christians living as God wants them to will sometimes face injustice. People striving to live morally good lives will, at times, be misunderstood, maligned, and even hated. How are they to face such hardships? Summarize Peter's answer in verses 19–20.*

- *Have you ever been mistreated because you did the right thing, the moral thing? Or do you know someone who endured such ill-treatment? Tell about the experience. What did it teach you (or the other person)?*

WORD WEALTH

Peter's call for submission in verse 18 is a directive for servants. The Greek word for *servant* that Peter uses is *oiketes*, referring to a household servant. James Strong defines this type of servant as "one of the family, of the household, but not necessarily born in the home."[12]

In Peter's day, a servant was typically a slave. The economic classes of the ancient world were basically the wealthy, small business owners (e.g., merchants, craftsmen, farmers, and day laborers), and servants or slaves. It's estimated that enslaved individuals and families made up a quarter to a third of the population of Italy.[13] Outside of Italy, the number of slaves varied widely, with some regions of the empire having far fewer than others.[14]

In the first century AD, slaves in the Roman Empire were granted many rights. For example, they could "worship as members of the extended family of their owner. They could marry." They were also "allowed to accumulate money of their own...that often could be used by them to purchase their freedom or to start a business when once they were...set free by their owners."[15]

Slaves worked as farmers, semiskilled labor, artisans, "architects, physicians, administrators, philosophers, grammarians, writers and teachers."[16] They also sometimes managed the estate or business of their owner. In other words, being a servant (or slave) in the Roman Empire was, in some circumstances, similar to the modern concept of employment.[17] While today's employees have more freedom and independence than Roman slaves did, many slaves received payment and other forms of compensation for services rendered, and when freed, which could occur in as little as seven years, "often...entered into business partnerships with their former owners."[18] Slaves were still regarded as property, not as free employees, but they could earn their owners' trust and admiration, which often had the effect of such slaves receiving more of an employee-like treatment.

- *What kind of employers have you experienced so far?*

- *If you had any who were difficult and demanding, how did you handle them, including when they might have treated you unfairly?*

- *What do you think about Peter's approach to dealing with mistreatment from an employer (vv. 18–20)? How do you think doing things Peter's way would go over with such an employer?*

The Example of Christ

Peter's rationale for enduring mistreatment is the example of Jesus Christ (v. 21).

- *When Jesus was verbally abused, how did he respond (v. 23)? How do you usually respond?*

- *When he suffered, what did he do (v. 23)? What do you typically do?*

- *What was his overall approach to mistreatment (v. 23)? What is yours?*

- *Given how Jesus handled mistreatment, what do you need to change in your response so you can be more like him?*

- *Peter then went on to tell about what Jesus did for us on the cross and how that has benefited us. Read 1 Peter 2:24–25 and answer the questions that follow:*

  What did Jesus accomplish for us on the cross?

  What was our spiritual condition when Jesus died for us?

  Who now watches over those of us who have put our faith in Jesus? How did Peter describe him?

  What does Jesus' work on the cross have to do with our seeing him as our example when dealing with mistreatment?

EXPERIENCE GOD'S HEART

- *Peter wrote his letter to "the chosen ones" (1:1), Christians. As a follower of Jesus Christ, what have you learned about yourself and God through times you have been mistreated for doing what is right? List at least two or three discoveries you've made.*

- *Would you now say that doing what is right is worth it, no matter how people treat you? Explain your answer.*

- *Read what Jesus said in Matthew 5:10–12. What did he say you will receive from God when you are persecuted for showing in your life that you love Jesus? Remember that Jesus told his disciples, "You show that you are my intimate friends when you obey all that I command you" (John 15:14). Our love for Jesus is shown through our obedience to him, which is always the right thing to do.*

SHARE GOD'S HEART

- *Do you know a fellow Christian who is suffering unjustly? What can you do to help that person?*

- *Christians in various countries suffer just because they identify with Jesus Christ and seek to live life his way. If you know of any of these situations, consider how you can reach out to this part of the body of Christ and help them alleviate or better endure their pain. If you are unaware of any such situations, check out Open Doors International (https://www.opendoors.org) or perhaps your local church to discover Christians who are suffering unjustly.*

Talking It Out

1. Jesus suffered unjustly. Even after his judge, Pontius Pilate, found him innocent of the charges leveled against him, Pilate eventually turned Jesus over to be executed to keep the crowd from turning into a riot (Matthew 27:11–26; Luke 23:1–25). How does Jesus' example help us when we face unjust treatment?

2. Jesus' suffering and death, which was evil, brought good: payment for all of humankind's sins. The crucifixion made divine forgiveness possible for all who accept Jesus by faith (John 3:16–18; Romans 3:23–26). How have you seen the evil of unjust suffering lead to good?

3. It's more than likely that you do not work as a servant, but it's fairly likely that you have a job (or did at one point in your life, if you are currently retired or are the boss yourself). What is one big takeaway that you have—related to Christian behavior in the workplace—in light of what you have learned in your study of 1 Peter 2:18–25?

LESSON 4

Virtuous Living

(1 Peter 3:1–12)

You can sum up marriage in many ways. And you can find countless books giving their best attempt at figuring out what makes for a successful marriage. For the apostle Peter, it's fair to say that marriage comes down to devotion and love.

Back in 1998, Oklahoma State's football coach, Bob Simmons, had just been named the NCAA Big 12 Conference's "Coach of the Year." He had just come off Oklahoma State's first winning season in a decade, turning around their entire program. Unbeknownst to everyone, however, Bob had been quietly suffering from failing kidneys and had reached the point where a kidney transplant was necessary. The biggest problem with that was, once his name was put on the donor list, he would be looking at a two-year wait.

Miraculously, he found a donor, had a successful surgery, and was back coaching in time for spring training. The donor? His wife, Linda. Linda, a nurse of twenty-five years at the time, and knowing all the risks, saw it as a God-ordained opportunity. She knew the decades of work her husband had put into landing his dream coaching job, and she was willing to make the sacrifice for him. Guided by the Lord's urging, she absolutely understood what she needed to do. According to a *Sports Illustrated* article covering this story, "It took the extraordinary devotion of his wife, Linda, to keep his dream—and him—alive."[19] Linda understood love and devotion.

- *When you think about marriage, what comes to mind? Do you think of a life of adventure with the love of your life, or do you think of hard work and heartache?*

- *Whose marriage do you most look up to? What, in your opinion, makes their marriage work?*

- *More than likely you know someone who has struggled in their marriage, and you probably know someone whose marriage ended in a separation or divorce. What do you see as the root causes of troubled marriages?*

Marital Counsel

Peter opened chapter 3 of his letter with a focus on marriage. First he spoke to wives (vv. 1–6), and then he directed his counsel to husbands (v. 7).

- *Before we dive into some of the details of these verses, let's become familiar with what they say.*

  Read what Peter advised wives to do and why (vv. 1–6). Then summarize his counsel here.

  Now read Peter's instruction to husbands (v. 7) and then summarize it here.

Wives: Character and Conduct

- *Reread verses 1–6, then answer the following questions:*

  What are wives to be (their character or virtue)?

What are wives to do?

What could be one of the outcomes of being this kind of wife?

WORD WEALTH

If you check the footnote on 1 Peter 3:1, you'll find that there is a slight difference in the translation of the word "devoted" when using the Greek text. The footnote reads, "The Greek is 'defer to the authority of your husbands' (patiently accept, submit)." It's worth noting that some other translations of the Bible render the same Greek word as "be subject" (ESV), "submit" (NIV), and "be submissive" (NKJV). A similar situation occurs in Ephesians 5:21–33, where Paul gave instruction on marriage. Ephesians 5:21 says that "out of reverence for Christ" we should "be supportive of each other in love." This prefaces Paul's opening counsel to wives to be "devoted to your husbands like you are tenderly devoted to our Lord" (v. 22). What TPT translates "supportive" and "devoted" some other translations render as "submitting" and "submit," respectively.

Why the different translation choices? While there are definitely some nuances to translating Scripture, a quick heart search will likely reveal the ease of accepting the concept of devotion much more easily than that of submission, despite the similar meaning when you consider the entire biblical context. Theologian John Piper, in speaking about submission, says, "Submission is a wider Christian virtue for all of us to pursue, and it has its unique and fitting expressions in various relationships."[20] Indeed, Peter's aim was to demonstrate that successful Christian living in a hostile world requires relating to others properly, whether you're conducting yourself in society in general (2:13–17), at your place of employment (vv. 18–25), or in your family as husband and wife (3:1–7).

- *Consider the following quote and also read Romans 12:2:*

> I'm convinced we must have *some* doctrine of submission (it is, after all, right there in the Bible) but don't think I'm alone in cringing a little bit when I hear the term "submit," especially in the context of marriage. When I hear "wives, submit to your own husbands," something happens in my mind or heart that I don't really like. I feel this immediate little bit of shame or rebellion or something. Submission feels old-fashioned. It feels like the kind of thing I may want to explain away like, "I know it looks like it says 'submit' but it doesn't really mean 'submit'." The problem is that it really does say "submit" and, as far as I can tell, really does mean it. There isn't one Bible translation that disagrees. So we just need to tackle it head-on.
>
> But what's happening? Why do I feel that little bit of rebellion or shame when I hear the word "submit?" I think it's proof that we as Christians are constantly battling worldliness. Worldliness is allowing our minds and hearts to be shaped by messages that come from outside the Bible. Remember Romans 12:2: "Do not be conformed to this world but be transformed by the renewing of your minds." Our minds are like Playdough and someone

> or something is always shaping them. Our lifelong battle is to ensure we are not being conformed to the thought-patterns of the world but are instead being transformed by the revelation of God. And in this area I think many Christians, myself included, have allowed worldliness to encroach just a little.
>
> The worldly thinking that constantly creeps into our minds is that our value and our dignity as people comes from our function or role, from what we do relative to other people. The Bible says something different. Your value and your dignity do not come from what you do but from *who you are*. And who are you? You are the one creature in all the world made in God's image! You do not gain value or dignity from your function, or your contribution, or your abilities. Your value and your dignity are intrinsic to you and equal to anyone else's because you are made in the image of God.
>
> Why is that important? Because a world that assigns value to function rebels against the idea of submission. It concludes that for a wife to submit to her husband means that she must have less value than her husband. This is false, but it's so often there in our minds and hearts.[21]

Bible scholar Mary J. Evans agreed, pointing out that Peter's call for wives to be submissive "does not…imply any inferiority." In fact, what Peter said here is better understood to refer to "the submissive *attitude* required of the wife rather than of any subordinate function." A wife's "attitude and demeanour" are in view here, not any suggestion that a wife is lesser than her husband.[22]

- *In your reading of 1 Peter 3:1–7, how does your understanding differ when you consider a wife being devoted to her husband versus a wife exercising a submissive attitude toward her husband? Does it make a difference? Why or why not?*

- *It's entirely likely that the concept of wives being devoted to their husbands (v. 1) and husbands treating their wives with tenderness (v. 7) is a completely acceptable ideal to you. And it really should be, especially if you are doing your best to model your life after the life of Jesus, who showed devotion and tenderness extremely well (e.g., praying with his friends in Luke 9:28–36 and ministering to the woman at the well in Samaria in John 1:1–26). List a few other times when Jesus demonstrated devotion and tenderness.*

- *Spend some time praying and asking the Lord to increase your understanding of devotion. Ask the Lord how you can better demonstrate devotion and show tenderness in your family relationships, particularly in your marriage relationship if you are married.*

DIGGING DEEPER

Along with counsel about character and devotion, Peter talked about a wife's outward appearance (1 Peter 3:3–4). To better understand his advice here, we need to get some of the cultural context of the ancient Roman world:

> In Greco-Roman culture, women who paid excessive attention to their appearance were viewed as promiscuous. Karen Jobes explains: "Outward adornments were often perceived as instruments of seduction (Philo, *On the Virtues* 7.39; Plutarch, *Advice* 140.30), and a woman's use of cosmetics was viewed as an attempt to deceive; both were unnecessary if a woman stayed at home (Xenophon, *Oeconomicus* 10.2)."
>
> If a woman was leaving the house to meet with fellow Christians for a Bible study, this would immediately arouse suspicion in her unbelieving husband.

> Plutarch wrote that "a wife ought not to make friends of her own, but to enjoy her husband's friends in common with him." In this culture, it was suspicious for a woman to have a network of friends other than her husband's....
>
> Therefore, what would an unbelieving husband think if his wife was dressing up with nice clothes and jewelry to frequent a Bible study? In this culture, he would assume that his wife was seeking to have an affair. This is why Peter tells wives to show such deference to their unbelieving husbands.[23]

- *Some of the early church fathers (Tertullian and Cyprian, for example) and some modern-day churches (e.g., some Seventh-day Adventists and some Apostolic Pentecostals) use 1 Peter 3:3–4 and 1 Timothy 2:9–10 as a means to prohibit certain types of dress or create a type of dress code for church. What's your opinion on how you should dress for church?*

- *What's your experience with regard to this topic? Did your parents make you "dress up" for church when you were a kid? What's the culture like at your current church when it comes to what people wear?*

- *What was Peter's point in addressing "outward adornment" (1 Peter 3:3–4)? Where did he say true beauty comes from?*

Husbands: Conduct and Perspective

- *Now reread 1 Peter 3:7 and the TPT notes for this verse. Then answer the questions that follow.*

  What are husbands supposed to do?

Why did Peter tell husbands to conduct themselves this way? What perspective should they have toward their wives?

If husbands fail to act appropriately toward their wives, what will happen in their relationship with God?

DIGGING DEEPER

In Peter's first-century world, women were regarded as weaker than men physically. For example, the Greek philosopher Aristotle wrote, "For Providence made man stronger and woman weaker, so that he in virtue of his manly prowess may be more ready to defend the home, and she, by reason of her timid nature, more ready to keep watch over it."[24] Peter likely had this well-known physical-strength difference in mind. But he also likely had in mind the weaker position women had legally and socially. Men had privileges and legal rights that women did not. This disparity led Peter to remind husbands that their wives were coheirs with them in Christ. Before the Lord, men and women were equal, and both were recipients of all the blessings Christ bestowed on his followers, including everlasting life. Therefore, husbands should treat their wives with tenderness and with honor.

What will happen if husbands fail to treat their wives as they should? What if they use their physical strength against their wives? What if they mistreat their wives, even if social and legal norms allow for it? Then, said Peter, their relationship with God will be stifled. Their prayers will be hindered (v. 7). As Bible scholar Karen Jobes put it,

> Peter points out that the well-being of the Christian household depends on the man recognizing the female as co-heir in Christ and living with her respectfully, even though he is the physically stronger and socially empowered male. In this way Peter delicately prohibits domestic violence in the Christian household.[25]

Jobes added, "Peter teaches that men whose authority runs roughshod over their women, even with society's full approval, will not be heard by God."[26]

EXPERIENCE GOD'S HEART

God wants us to love one another whether we are married or single (1 Peter 3:8). In a marriage, though, life is shared closely and intimately—more so in that relationship than in any other. Tenderness, respect, encouragement, affection, honor, deference, sacrifice, gentleness, courage, and so much more are needed to help a marriage to develop, deepen, and endure. God wants couples to grow together in him.

- *If you are married, how have you loved and matured together?*

- *Is Christ central to your relationship? If so, how? If not, why?*

- *If you are single, what do you think about Peter's marital counsel? Does it resonate with your understanding of marriage? Why or why not?*

- *If you are a single woman and would like to marry, how do you think you should treat your future husband? What do you think loving him would look like and feel like to him?*

- *If you are a single man who would like to marry one day, how do you think you should treat your future wife? What do you think loving her would look like and feel like to her?*

Living and Loving Together

God's heart for the church—for how believers are to interact with one another—is revealed in 1 Peter 3:8–9, and it is important to understand the relationship you are to have with other believers. If those relationships aren't solid, you won't be as effective in your ability to share God's love with others.

- *There are nine virtues that Peter detailed in verses 8 and 9. These virtues are to be the standard for how Christians are to interact with one another. For each virtue listed below, define it in the context of how you are to interact with others, especially in your relationship with your church family. (Hint: you can define each virtue with a few words, a phrase, a complete sentence, or an example from your own life.)*

    1) "Live in harmony"

    2) "Demonstrate affectionate love"

3) Demonstrate "sympathy"

4) Show "kindness toward other believers"

5) Be described by humility

6) Love dearly

7) "Never retaliate"

8) Never insult others

9) Bless others

- *Which of these virtues are a part of you and what you do?*

- *Which virtues seem rare or even absent from you and how you conduct your life?*

- *Ask the Lord to further strengthen and mature the virtues that are now part of your life. Then ask him to develop within you the virtues that seem more distant from your life. You may find that choosing one to work on and practice will be more feasible at this time in your life.*

Good Versus Evil

After speaking about wives and husbands and then about how believers are to live with one another, Peter returned to the theme that has permeated his letter: good versus evil. He drew from Psalm 34, which he saw as supplying scriptural support for what he had just said about how to handle people who treat us wrongly or insult us.

- *Read 1 Peter 3:10–12 and then answer the following questions:*

  What wrongs should we reject and refuse to practice?

  What rights—good actions—should we pursue and cultivate?

  Why should we pursue what is good over what is evil?

Whether or not we win someone to Christ because of our caring conduct, Peter wanted us to know that God's heart for us is to "always turn from what is wrong and cultivate what is good" (v. 11). We may suffer for doing the good, but that should not deter us. We must always remember what Jesus said about those who follow him: "Your lives light up the world....So don't hide your light! Let it shine brightly before others, so that your commendable works will shine as light upon them, and then they will give their praise to your Father in heaven" (Matthew 5:14, 16). People know who we are—Christians—by what we do. Words matter, but actions matter more. We share God's heart—his love for others—by how we live, which includes our words and our deeds. And our deeds verify or undermine our words.

- *What do you think about how you're doing when it comes to being a light for Christ and what is good?*

- *When you hear from other people (Christians or non-Christians), what do they say about you? Do they see good? Do they see Christlikeness?*

- *What do you need to change in your life so that you will be the light Christ talked about? We share God's heart by being a light to others.*

Talking It Out

1. Given the teachings in this chapter of 1 Peter, how can Christians better serve their families and their churches? How can *you* better serve in your role as a member of your family and your church?

2. At the time Peter was writing, Christians were in serious peril. You are unlikely in a similar situation. However, you have and will face trials in your life. Think of a recent situation that has been difficult for you. How can you overcome the challenges of your situation by applying the virtues and actions that Peter listed in verses 8–12?

LESSON 5

Beyond Intimidation and Fear

(1 Peter 3:13–4:19)

In his book *Blue Like Jazz*, Donald Miller recounted a story he heard while at a concert. Basically, in between songs, the musician told a story about a friend, a Navy SEAL whose team was participating in a hostage rescue mission. The SEALs breached the building, finding all the hostages huddled up in the corner. When the SEALs called out to them, letting them know they were safe and being rescued, the hostages wouldn't move. The SEALs didn't know what to do because there were too many of them to carry out. But Miller's friend had an idea. He put down his gun, took off his helmet, and sat down by the hostages. He put his arms around them and waited for them to realize he was one of them. Then he simply said, "Will you follow us?" And they did.[27]

Fear can paralyze us. And fear often comes as the result of intimidation. These hostages had been intimidated by their captors. Likewise, kids can be intimidated by bullies, employees by bosses, lawyers by judges, a spouse by an abusive mate, and a pastor by an overbearing congregant. We need not be locked away to experience fear and feel threatened.

Peter's first recipients were either undergoing suffering or saw it coming their way. Peter wanted to help them understand why this was occurring and how they could handle it. In 1 Peter 3:13 to the end of chapter 4, he brought up two common responses to their suffering, whether it had already arrived for some of his readers or seemed for others to be on the horizon. These responses were intimidation and bewilderment. In the midst of his counsel, he also urged his readers to make sure that any suffering they faced was due to them living as Christ followers rather than to them living as lawbreakers or meddlesome neighbors.

Facing Intimidation

Intimidation is the first response to the fear of suffering that Peter addressed. He started by posing a question and then quoting from a psalm.

- *What question did Peter ask (1 Peter 3:13)?*

- *Given what Peter already said about living God's way, what about that kind of living would make it unreasonable for someone to hurt a faithful believer?*

- *Now, what did Peter say believers who "suffer for doing what is right" (v. 14) would receive for their pain?*

- *Peter did not say here what this blessing is, but what do you suppose it is given what he has said in his letter already?*

- *What is the thrust of the passage from Isaiah 8:12–13 that Peter summarized (1 Peter 3:14)?*

- *How should we handle those who try to intimidate us (vv. 15–16)?*

- *What did Peter mean by "maintaining a clear conscience," and what will that force our intimidators to do and experience?*

The Greek word translated "explain" in verse 15 is *apologia*, and it means "defense" or "reasoned reply." In Peter's day,

> [*apologia*] was often used of the argument for the defense in a court of law and though the word may have the idea of a judicial interrogation in which one is called to answer for the manner in which he has exercised his responsibility..., the word can also mean an informal explanation or defense of one's position (s. 1 Cor. 9:3; 2 Cor. 7:11) and the word would aptly describe giving an answer to the skeptical, abusive, or derisive inquiries of ill-disposed neighbors.[28]

One way to handle intimidation over being a Christian is to provide a clear explanation of what you believe and a reasoned defense of why you believe it. When you can engage someone with this level of understanding of your faith, you will not fear, and you will not feel intimidated. You will speak with confidence while showing compassion. You will stand with conviction while behaving respectfully.[29]

- *Have you ever stood your ground in defense of your faith? If so, what happened? What did you learn from the experience?*

- *If you have never given another person an explanation or defense of "the hope living within you" (1 Peter 3:15), why is this so? What, if anything, is holding you back?*

Better to Suffer

Peter then made a surprising claim: "It is better to suffer for doing good, if it is in God's plan, than for doing evil" (v. 17). We might say that it's better not to suffer at all—to avoid it altogether! But Peter went in a different direction. If we are going to suffer, if it is in God's plan for us to suffer, then it's far better for us to suffer for doing what's good than to suffer for doing what's evil. Can suffering be part of God's plan, even for his children, for his followers? Yes, it can, and it has been so.

- *Who suffered for us, and what did he accomplish through that suffering (v. 18)?*

- *How have you benefited from what Jesus suffered?*

A Prophetic Picture

The rest of 1 Peter 3 has been difficult to interpret for centuries. Rather than predispose you to think of the passage one way or another, it's best for you to familiarize yourself with it and work through it on your own.

- *Read 1 Peter 3:18–22, paying particular attention to verses 19–22. Then return to verse 19. In your estimation, who does "He" refer to at the start of verse 19? The subject of verse 18 is Christ, but the more immediate referent for "He" in verse 19 is the Spirit. Do you think verse 19 is talking about Christ or the Spirit?*

- *What is "the spiritual realm" (v. 19)?*

- *Who are "the spirits in prison" (v. 20)?*

- *How does the mention of Noah's story connect to the imprisoned spirits and their disobedience (v. 20)?*

- *Now read the footnotes for verses 19 and 20 in TPT. What light do they shed on the interpretation of these verses?*

- *Noah's story is, according to the apostle Peter, "a prophetic picture of the immersion that now saves you" (v. 21)? What immersion is this?*

- *Does water baptism play a role in our salvation? Why or why not?*

- *Where is Jesus now, and what kind of authority does he have (v. 22)?*

DIGGING DEEPER

Verses 18–22 form a unit of thought in Peter's letter. Verse 18 centers on the suffering Jesus Christ endured to bring Peter's readers "near to God." Their salvation was made possible by Jesus' death on the cross and the victory over death that came about by his resurrection from the dead. Verse 19 shows that Jesus' victory even extended to the disobedient and imprisoned angels ("spirits") who were unbound during Noah's day (Genesis 6:1–4).[30] Due to the terrible corruption of humanity at this time in history (6:5, 11–12), God chose to carry out his judgment through an expansive and destructive flood. In his mercy, however, he chose to save one man and his family, for God found Noah to be "a godly man of integrity" (v. 9). God instructed Noah to build an ark in which he and his family—"eight souls" in all (1 Peter 3:20; see Genesis 6:18)—would be spared from the judgment to come. Peter compared this biblical account to the water baptism of believers. Noah and his family were spared divine judgment from flood waters—waters that cleansed the earth of human corruption. They are a "picture" of what water baptism by immersion does for those who depend on Jesus for their salvation (1 Peter 3:21). Water baptism does not cleanse the body of dirt, but the act does express and confirm what has already occurred in the believer—namely, the cleansing of one's conscience so it can now be called "good" (v. 21). This is the salvation that Jesus Christ secured through his own resurrection from the dead (v. 21). This same Jesus is now the Authority of authorities, seated next to God the Father in the heavenly realm (v. 22).

Because Christ secures the believer's salvation, Peter's readers can rest assured that through Jesus Christ they, too, will have victory over their suffering. With this Lord on their side, they have no one to fear. They will have the ultimate victory.

Preparing for Suffering

The main point of 1 Peter 4 is found in the first verse: "Since Christ, though innocent, suffered in his flesh for you, now you also must be a prepared soldier." Prepared for what? For potential suffering due to a Christian's choice to follow Jesus.

- *What must our mindset be as prepared soldiers (v. 1)? Check out Matthew 16:24 to see what Jesus told his disciples they were to prepare for and how.*

- *How are we to live the rest of our earthly lives (1 Peter 4:2)? What are we to pursue, and what are we to avoid?*

- *What marks the life of unbelievers? What do they typically love (v. 3)?*

- *What do unbelievers find so astonishing about believers, and how do they treat believers as a result (v. 4)?*

- *What will unbelievers one day face (v. 5)?*

- *Will the unbelievers' judgment on Christians be treated as final in the afterlife (v. 6)? Why or why not?*

- *How does what Peter said in verses 1–6 influence your view of suffering in this life? Does it give you hope and strength to stand firm in Christ? Why or why not?*

- *Peter seemed to draw a line in the sand here: choose Jesus and suffering or choose sin. To what extent have you experienced such a choice in your life? In what areas of your life have you demonstrated that you are done with human desires? In what areas do you still need work?*

- *How does the reality that you have eternal life to look forward to encourage you when faced with persecution, suffering, or other kinds of trials?*

EXPERIENCE GOD'S HEART

God's love for you is intense; in fact, it's so intense that it covers over all your sins (v. 8). Peter encouraged that level of love—an intense love—as Christians live out their relationships with others. He also reminded Christians that God will never fail them (v. 19).

- *When you experience God's love for you—realizing that all your sin is covered, "for love will be a canopy over a multitude of sins" (v. 8)—how should that reflect itself in how you treat others, especially in your interactions with "foreigners," or strangers (v. 9)?*

- *Peter continued talking about suffering in the last part of chapter 4. What was his particular instruction for believers when "life gets extremely difficult, with many tests" (v. 12)? How does his solution reflect God's heart for those who suffer (vv. 12–14)?*

SHARE GOD'S HEART

When Christians serve others, they do so under God's grace, receiving "grace gifts" (v. 10). Peter gave the example of having the gifts of speaking and serving in verse 11. He talked about using the gift of speaking to allow God's words to be the words that are spoken, and he also talked about using the gift of serving to passionately serve others with God's strength.

- *What do you consider to be your gifts? How do you use them in serving others?*

- *How can you "glorify God" (v. 16) when you are put through "many tests" (v. 12) or are "insulted" (v. 14)? How should your response align with sharing God's heart in the midst of adversity?*

- *How can maintaining a positive witness in the face of persecution or suffering impact how others perceive your faith in God and also God himself—especially when those "others" are unbelievers?*

Talking It Out

1. Peter wanted to make sure that his readers suffered for what was good, not for what was bad. Read his counsel on this in 1 Peter 4:15–19. For what should we not suffer? But if we suffer because we are Christians, how should we regard that and how should we endure it?

2. For Christians, trials purify, creating in us an "authentic faith" that "will result in even more praise, glory, and honor when Jesus the Anointed One is revealed" in the last days (1:7). In fact, divine judgment starts with us (4:17), but not judgment as punishment for sin since Jesus has taken that on for us (Romans 3:21–24). Our judgment is a judgment that purifies and refines us, removing the corruption that still lingers in our lives (Malachi 3:1–6). But Peter tells us that even with all of this going for us, we will still be "barely saved" (1 Peter 4:18). If that's true for us, what will be the fate of "the wicked and godless" (v. 18), of those "who refuse to obey the gospel of God" (v. 17)? Discuss how the fate of unbelievers should influence us.

LESSON 6

Be Humble...Hang Back

(1 Peter 5)

As you can probably imagine, countries located in the Southern Hemisphere, where it doesn't snow much, don't tend to dominate international winter sports. In fact, the first Olympic gold medal by an athlete from a country located in the Southern Hemisphere was in 2002, when an Australian speed skater named Steven Bradbury managed to win a gold medal in the men's short track, thousand-meter speed skating event. Now, Bradbury was a solid skater, doing well (and medaling) on the international stage in previous years, despite having faced a good deal of adversity in his career (a broken neck from trying to avoid crashing into an opponent and more than one hundred stitches from having an opponent's skate go straight through his leg).

The story of his gold medal performance is quite revealing. Bradbury, upon making the finals, knew full well he wasn't fast enough to defeat his opponents. So he decided to hang in the back of the pack. His hope was that a crash might occur, allowing him to place in the event. His strategy paid off in a huge way. On the last corner of the last lap, his four opponents got tangled up and crashed, allowing him to cross the finish line first for the gold medal.[31] Bradbury had an amazing race and victory, largely due to his humility and strategy.

- *Have you ever participated in an event where you knew you had no chance of winning? What was your attitude before, during, and after competing?*

- *In 1 Peter 5, Peter called upon leaders to lead with heart, to serve, and to remain humble. Who are some leaders you admire? How would you describe their character? What qualities do they exhibit in their roles as leaders?*

In the first several verses of 1 Peter 5, Peter brought up elders. You likely have leaders in your church who are called elders. Many churches are even managed by elders, with the lead pastor sometimes serving as one of the elders or as the chief elder. In the first century, however, elders had a different relationship to local churches.

As Luke, the writer of Acts, informed us, the early church began in Jerusalem. Here the leaders were the apostles (minus Paul, who had not yet converted to Christianity; Acts 1:12–26) and, in a short period of time, deacons (6:1–6). Later we learn that elders had become part of the church's leadership (11:30). We don't know when elders were initially added to the church's structure of government. But before Luke ever mentioned Christian elders, he had already referred to Jewish elders (4:5, 8, 23; 6:12). Then, after first bringing up Christian elders, Luke continued to mention Jewish ones (23:14; 24:1; 25:15). According to minister Kevin Giles, "This [pattern] suggests that [Luke] assumes that Jewish and Christian elders are much the same phenomenon."[32] In other words, they shared similar roles and responsibilities.

So who were the elders in first-century Judaism, and what did they do? Well, they were usually the older men and women, the ones in their senior years. Some of these individuals became community leaders. They arose to such a position "by being the son of a village or clan leader, by wisdom, by wealth or other things that gave prestige, and in rabbinic times by knowledge of the law."[33] Also, they were *not* officials in the synagogues. They were involved in synagogue assemblies "as older respected men, reading the Scriptures, in some cases commenting on the readings, and leading the gathering in prayer, but they were not office-bearers in the synagogues."[34]

What about *Christian* elders? Who were they, and what did they do? From the information we have in the New Testament, Christian elders also appear to be community leaders, like their Jewish counterparts. They oversaw all the churches in their city or region.

Now churches were not stand-alone buildings reserved for Christian worship. The early churches were typically house churches; Christians met in people's homes, not in buildings set aside as worship centers (Acts 2:46; 8:3; 12:12–17; 16:15, 34, 40; 18:7; Romans 16:5, 23; 1 Corinthians 14:23; 16:19; Colossians 4:15; Philemon 2; 2 John 1, 10). Historian and sociologist D. J. Tidball said that these "households were not the private residences of today but were most likely to be large houses which provided shops at the front and living accommodations at the rear. There would also have been room for workshops and living quarters for dependents and visitors."[35] Houses in which Christians met had room for about fifty people or less, and the leaders of each of these houses appeared to be the homeowners. As Giles stated, "Neither apostles, elders nor prophets are drawn as leaders of house churches. It seems rather that the owner of the home presided when believers assembled, as did the 'ruler of a synagogue,' and people present contributed freely as the Spirit led."[36] Just as a synagogue assembly often occurred in a house, so did a Christian assembly. And just as the Jewish homeowner was one of the leaders (if not the presiding leader) of a Jewish assembly, so the Christian homeowner(s) served as the leader of his or her respective Christian gathering.

The leaders of a house church were called bishops (Greek: *episkopoi*). New Testament scholar C. G. Kruse said, "Bishops were the hosts of the house churches and they exercised a supervisory role over the church meeting in their houses. Elders [Greek: *presbyteroi*] were leaders in the Christian community, but were not necessarily hosts of house churches as well."[37] Elders, then, had oversight over all of the house churches that met in a particular city or region. For example, in Acts 20:17, Luke noted how Paul invited "the elders of the church in Ephesus" to meet him in Miletus, a city thirty-six miles south of Ephesus.[38]

> Paul first visited the large and important city of Ephesus in AD 52 (Acts 18:18–21), where he stayed "for a considerable time" (Acts 18:18), returning on his third missionary journey and staying this time for over two years (Acts 19:8–10). Luke makes it clear that Paul's ministry in Ephesus was very successful. Many people became Christians and many house churches were established. At some point we may presume that he made sure there was citywide Christian communal leadership; elders were appointed. Paul invites these elders to meet with him at Miletus.[39]

Toward the end of speaking to these elders, Paul charged them to be "true shepherds over all the flock," reminding them that God had "appointed" them to "guard and oversee the churches that belong to Jesus" (Acts 20:28). According to Paul, then, the functions of these elders were oversight and protection of all of the house churches in Ephesus under their care.

Now let's see what Peter had to say.

Elder Leadership

Peter had already identified himself as an apostle (1 Peter 1:1). But as he opened chapter 5, he called himself an elder, a community church leader (5:1).

- *What else did Peter say about himself in 5:1?*

- *Was Peter exalting himself or humbling himself? Or is there another option? Explain your answer.*

- *Peter then spoke to his "fellow elders" (v. 1). What did he charge them to do (v. 2)?*

- *In what characteristic way did Peter want these elders to carry out their role and responsibilities (vv. 2–3)?*

- *Why did Peter say that elders should lead as he proposed (v. 4)?*

Young Members

Peter was not only concerned about senior, mature leaders. He had counsel to give to the younger crowd—those under the leadership of the elders and those who might move into leadership roles as they matured in Christ.

- *What was Peter's counsel to the younger members of the Asian churches (v. 5)?*

- *Why do you think it's important for young people to pursue humility over pride? How does the virtue of humility set up a young person for success later in life, especially where leadership is concerned?*

Counsel for All

Keeping young people in mind, Peter provided counsel for all who follow Jesus Christ by faith.

- *How should all of us relate to God, and how will God respond to us (vv. 6–7)?*

- *When it comes to handling our greatest enemy, Satan, what should we do and why (vv. 8–9, including the footnotes for these verses)?*

- *What will God do to support us in our resistance to Satan and our endurance through suffering (vv. 10–11)?*

Letter Wrap-Up

In the last three verses of 1 Peter, the apostle wrapped up his letter to the believers he addressed living in Asia, what we know today as Turkey (1:1).

- *Who wrote this letter, and who acted as the writer's assistant (5:12)?*

- *How did Peter describe his assistant (v. 12)? Do you think you could rely on such a person? Why or why not?*

- *What did Peter say was his central reason for penning his letter (v. 12)?*

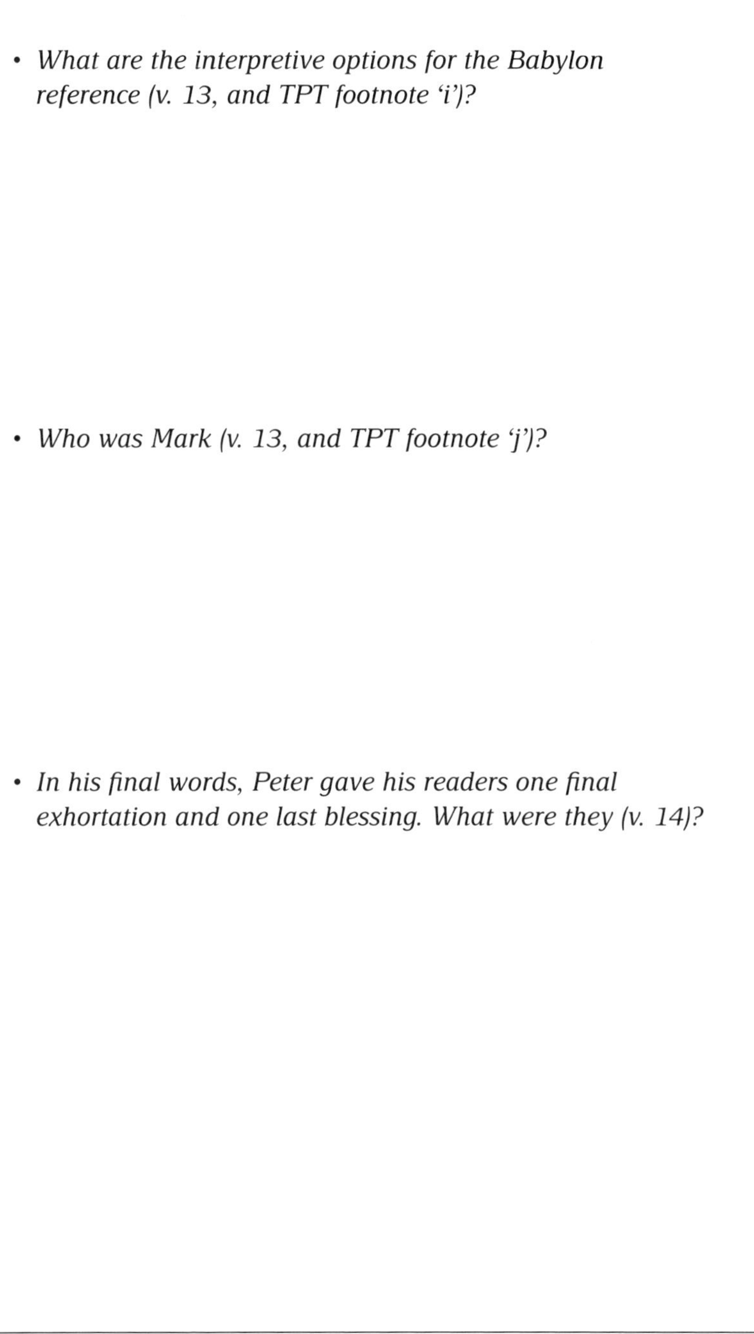

- *What are the interpretive options for the Babylon reference (v. 13, and TPT footnote 'i')?*

- *Who was Mark (v. 13, and TPT footnote 'j')?*

- *In his final words, Peter gave his readers one final exhortation and one last blessing. What were they (v. 14)?*

EXPERIENCE GOD'S HEART

- *If you had to zero in on an overarching point of 1 Peter 5, what would it be? What does it have to do with God's heart for you?*

SHARE GOD'S HEART

- *Consider Peter's instructions and thoughts on leadership and the pursuit of humility in chapter 5. In what ways can these principles help foster a loving and supportive church community?*

Talking It Out

1. What was Peter's advice in chapter 5, verse 8 regarding facing spiritual opposition? What are some ways Christians can strengthen their faith in order to effectively resist Satan?

2. What is God's promise to you in chapter 5, verse 10? How can that promise comfort and strengthen you in times of trials and suffering?

3. Throughout 1 Peter, the apostle called on believers to live holy lives, thereby reflecting their identity as God's people. Discuss what holiness looks like in practical terms, especially in the context of the world in which you live.

4. Peter talked a lot about suffering in 1 Peter. Overall, it's fair to say that, for Peter, suffering had a purpose in refining faith and demonstrating the authenticity of one's relationship with Christ. Discuss how suffering can be a means of growth—and a powerful testimony—in your life.

LESSON 7

2 Peter: Peter's Ladder

(2 Peter 1:1–11)

Peter's second letter (2 Peter 1:1; 3:1) reflects the love and grace God showed Peter throughout his life. For its recipients in the last half of the first century—and for readers today—2 Peter serves as a treasure trove of revelation about the triumphant grace and lavish love that Christians receive from God.

Peter's second letter also carries with it an atmosphere of urgency, because an increase of false teachings had infiltrated and begun to influence the churches to which he wrote. This great concern weighed on Peter, for he knew that his days on earth were coming to an end (1:13–15). Clearing the air with regard to the meaning of God's grace—that it is a cause for diligently holding on to faith and not a cause for living an immoral life—Peter exhorted Christians to live virtuously as they looked forward to Christ's return.

- *Recall a few of Peter's greatest moments, along with some of the not-so-great ones. For example, Peter's confession of Jesus as the promised Messiah was a great moment (Matthew 16:13–20), and Peter denying that he knew Jesus three times was definitely not one of his best moments (Luke 22:54–62). Given what you know about Peter's past, how important do you think was his experience with God's grace? In what ways do you imagine it shaped him?*

- *Place yourself in Peter's shoes (or sandals). If you were surrounded by persecution and the very real potential of martyrdom, and you wanted to write down some instructions, give some advice, or provide some encouragement to fellow believers, what would be at the top of your list?*

Authorship, Date, and Audience

In the early centuries of the church, some Christian leaders were not confident that 2 Peter had been composed by the apostle Peter. After all, the letter's writing style seemed somewhat different from that of 1 Peter. Plus, the letter had no long line of tradition that could be clearly traced back to the time of the apostles.[40] Matters such as these led some of the early church fathers to contest the letter's authenticity, putting it into the category of *antilegomena*, or questioned books. (The other books in this group were Hebrews, James, Jude, 2 and 3 John, and Revelation, with each one questioned for different reasons.) Nevertheless, 2 Peter, along with the other contested books, was eventually embraced as Holy Scripture. The issues raised over it were adequately addressed. By the latter part of the fourth century, all of the current twenty-seven books of the New Testament had been acknowledged as canonical Scripture by Athanasius (the bishop of Alexandria) in 367, the synod of Hippo in 393, the synod of Carthage in 397, and the Council of Carthage in 419.[41]

Peter wrote his second letter around the same time as his first (AD 64–66). And although Peter doesn't mention a specific audience in this second letter as he did in his first, it's fair to say that since he mentions 2 Peter as the "second letter" he has penned to his audience, this readership was the same as those mentioned at the start of his first letter. If this is so, then the first readers of 2 Peter were scattered Christians throughout Asia Minor (modern-day Turkey).

- *Read through TPT's introduction to 2 Peter, especially the section "Author and Audience." Jot down some things that stand out to you as you read these pages.*

Major Themes

You'll encounter four overarching themes as you delve into 2 Peter: (1) the triune nature of God, (2) the corrupt nature of humanity and God's deliverance, (3) how to live in the "last days," and (4) false teachers.

- *Read the entirety of 2 Peter; it's just three chapters long.*

1) The Triune Nature of God

Just like in 1 Peter, Peter concerned his readers with the need to understand God's triune nature. Peter emphasized that God the Father is the one who inspired the prophets, the one who declared the true nature of Jesus (2 Peter 1:17–21), and the one in charge of the coming judgment upon humanity (3:10–12). Peter told us that God the Holy Spirit is key to the interpretation of Scripture and to its inspiration (1:20–21). But Peter's primary focus is on God the Son, Jesus Christ. Peter certainly has Jesus in the foreground of the entirety of 2 Peter, referring to him throughout the epistle as Lord (1:2, 11, 14, 16; 2:20; 3:2, 18), Messiah (1:11; 2:20), and Savior (1:1, 11; 2:20; 3:2, 18), for example.

- *Why do you think it matters that Peter revealed the triune nature of God in this epistle?*

- *Consider another theme of 2 Peter: false teaching. Why is it so important that Peter focused on the divine nature of Jesus when talking about false teaching?*

2) The Corrupt Nature of Humanity and God's Deliverance

Peter revealed two important things about humanity in 2 Peter. First, "corrupt desires" pervade the hearts of those in the world (1:4). And second, humans have the ability to escape the corruption of the world because of their access to true deliverance. Indeed, Peter revealed the truth of salvation: that its source is the recognition and acknowledgment of Jesus as the Savior (v. 3).

- *According to his own testimony (Matthew 16:13–20), Peter proclaimed Jesus as the Messiah. And while he probably wasn't the only one to realize it at the time, he definitely was bold enough to proclaim the truth of it. What has been your experience of knowing Jesus and his goodness (2 Peter 1:3)?*

3) How to Live in the Last Days

It's likely that Peter, the other apostles, and the various early Christian communities initially thought that Jesus would return during their lifetimes. Peter alluded to this in 1 Peter 4:7, and Paul seemed to believe it to be the case in 1 Thessalonians 4:13–18. Peter spent nearly the entirety of 2 Peter 3 talking about being ready for Jesus' return.

- *Why do you think proper living and the inevitable return of Jesus are so interconnected for Peter? (Think of it this way: If you knew Jesus was coming back tomorrow, how would you act?)*

4) False Teachers

Warning of false teachers and their teachings is clearly one of the main reasons that Peter wrote this letter. There were already many false teachings becoming prominent in Peter's day, within only a few decades after Jesus' resurrection. Peter was particularly concerned with those who teach against the sovereign nature of the Lord.

- *Why do you think calling out teachers and their teachings that question Jesus' sovereignty is such an important topic for Peter?*

Peter's Ladder

Peter was sure of his faith—he had to have been. After all, he went from leaving his work as a fisherman to following Jesus to walking on water (albeit briefly) to becoming a leader of the apostles to denying he even knew Jesus to (again) becoming a leader (this time of the entire early Christian church). How did he make all of this work? He relied on God's grace, his faith in Jesus, and Jesus' Spirit-provided empowerment.

In 2 Peter 1:3–4, Peter expressed why he was able to grasp the concept of God's grace and be content and confident that he could stand against a hostile world: "Everything we could ever need for life and godliness has already been deposited in us by his divine power… [so that] we can experience partnership with the divine nature."

- *Peter's phrase in verse 4, "partnership with the divine nature," is yet another way to describe how those of us in Christ are, by the Spirit's power, becoming more and more like Jesus. We are being made into his likeness, his image. Just as he perfectly images the invisible God, he is working within us—God's image-bearers—to make us like himself so we can image God more fully. To better grasp this, look up the following passages. Next to each one, note what it reveals about how we are becoming more like Jesus Christ, the one who is "the exact expression of God's true nature—his mirror image" (Hebrews 1:3).*

  1 Corinthians 15:42–49

  Colossians 3:8–11

Philippians 3:20–21

When good leaders are tested, they rise to the occasion and they often receive great insight and particular revelations. For Peter, in the face of an uncertain future and a corrupt world that seemed to have more than a few false teachers, the absolute answer for him seems to be standing resolute in his faith. Peter encouraged Christians to supplement their faith step-by-step with a series of virtues (2 Peter 1:5–7).

- *For each virtue listed (indicated by bold text), offer your own definition of the particular virtue, along with a practical example from your own life.*

1. *Add **goodness** to faith:*

2. *Add **understanding** to goodness:*

3. *Add **self-control** to understanding:*

4. Add ***patient endurance*** *to self-control:*

5. Add ***godliness*** *to patient endurance:*

6. Add ***mercy toward fellow Christians*** *to godliness:*

7. Add ***unending love*** *to mercy toward fellow Christians:*

EXPERIENCE GOD'S HEART

God's heart in 2 Peter 1:1–11 is that you would come to the full realization that he has "claimed you as his own" (v. 10). Peter's intent here was certainly to bring joy to those weary of heart.

- *Peter started out his second letter stating that "everything we could ever need for life and godliness…was lavished upon us through the rich experience of knowing him who has called us by name" (v. 3). When you think of yourself as "lavished upon" and "called" by God himself, how does that make you feel?*

- *What does it mean to you that God has "claimed" you (v. 10)?*

- *What assurances does God give you as you seek after him and strive to live a faithful and fruitful life (adding virtues to your faith)? For a hint, see verses 10–11.*

SHARE GOD'S HEART

- *How can your knowledge of the promises that God has for you in 2 Peter 1:10–11 influence your attitude in your day-to-day life, especially with regard to how you interact with others? And what does the manner in which you interact with others reveal about your knowledge of those promises?*

- *Peter stated that growth in virtues ensures fruitfulness in the knowledge of Christ (v. 8). How can this fruitfulness be a reflection of God's heart for you to make a positive impact in your local church and your local community?*

- *In what ways can the promise of a triumphant entrance into the eternal kingdom influence how you live out your faith today (v. 11)?*

Talking It Out

1. Look back at the list of virtues in verses 5–7. Which of the virtues listed do you find most challenging to cultivate? Why do you think that is? What are a few ways in which you could work on increasing your implementation of at least one of the virtues that you find challenging?

2. Do a quick assessment. How is your spiritual growth? Do you feel that you are more virtuous now compared to when you first became a Christian?

3. How can Peter's "ladder of virtue" help you build resilience when you face temptations or trials?

4. Two of the themes of 2 Peter have to do with living in a corrupt world and how to live well in the face of the last days. Discuss some practical ways (based upon your reading and study of 2 Peter 1:1–11) that you can keep from stumbling (v. 10).

LESSON 8

Truth Confirmed

(2 Peter 1:12–21)

How do you know that something is true?

Do you have to experience it yourself? If so, then what could you ever know about things that you have never experienced or may never have the chance to experience?

Perhaps you accept only those truth claims that your five senses (touch, smell, hearing, sight, and taste) can confirm. If so, then you could never know anything in the past that occurred before your birth. Plus, you could not know anything that was abstract, such as the meaning of love, justice, or the law.

Maybe your test for truth is based solely on what other sources tell you is true. If that's so, then how do you handle conflicting and even contradictory claims that come from those sources?

People make truth claims all the time. How can we know which ones are true and which ones are false? The apostle Peter wanted his readers to know the truth about Jesus, his teachings, and his provisions for them. And Peter strove to distance the truth of what he said from legends of the day—stories that may excite and intrigue but are factually false (2 Peter 1:16). In the process, he explained how a truth claim he already believed was magnificently confirmed to him and those with him. Peter shared his experience of Jesus with his readers and provided other evidences as well so they could be better established in their faith. Let's carefully consider what he wrote.

Truths to Remember

- *Peter began this section of his letter by telling his readers that he would keep reminding them of "these truths" (1:12). What truths is he talking about? (Hint: look to the previous verses for your answer.)*

- *Is it helpful to you to be reminded of truths you already know? Why or why not?*

- *Why did Peter provide his readers with such a reminder of various truths (vv. 13–15)?*

- *Have you ever had a loved one, a mentor, or someone else in your life remind you of truths that they didn't want you to forget after their passing? If so, who was it, and what truths did this person want you to never forget?*

The Incarnate Lord: One of Those Truths

Peter then turned to remind these Christians of another truth he had taught them—namely, that Jesus was, in fact, the Lord and Messiah (vv. 11, 16). Jesus was the very one that the prophets of old spoke about. And he came in "power" and revealed his divine nature and relationship with the heavenly Father in "magnificence and splendor" (v. 16).

- *How did Peter encounter Jesus' self-revelation? Which of his senses does he emphasize (vv. 16–18)?*

- *Did Peter experience this revelation of Jesus alone or were others with him (vv. 16, 18)? What is the textual evidence for your answer?*

- *What did Peter see happen (vv. 16–17)?*

- *What did Peter hear (vv. 17–18)?*

- *Where were Peter and his companions when this event occurred (v. 18)?*

- *To get a fuller account of Jesus' transfiguration, read each of the following passages and jot down what you learn from each one. Do all of them report the same details, or do you find some additional information in any of them?*

  Matthew 17:1–13

  Mark 9:2–13

  Luke 9:28–36

The Divine Word Confirmed

Peter's readers clearly knew of the Scriptures, the very word of God, for he told them to "stay focused on it" (2 Peter 1:19). What's telling is the connection Peter made between the written word and Jesus' transfiguration.

- *Whose "confirming voice" served to make "the prophetic word…more reliable and fully validated" (v. 19)?*

- *What was it that this voice said about Jesus during his transfiguration (v. 17)?*

- *How does the fact that Jesus is God's Son verify or confirm the reliability of the prophetic word of God? For help, see the TPT footnotes 'b' and 'c' for 1:19.*

"The phrase *prophetic word*, or 'word of prophecy,' when found in Christian writing through the second century is used only for Old Testament Scriptures."[42] It was these writings that spoke of a Messiah who would

- *be born of a virgin in Bethlehem (Isaiah 7:14; Micah 5:2–3);*
- *spring from the royal tribe of Judah (Genesis 49:10);*
- *trust in God the Father from his birth onward (Psalm 22:10);*
- *be God's Son (Psalm 89:26);*
- *be deity, "Lord" even to King David (Psalm 110:1);*
- *be a branch from David on whom God's Spirit would rest and empower (Isaiah 11:1–2);*
- *have a forerunner named John (Isaiah 40:3; Malachi 3:1);*
- *be anointed with God's Spirit to preach the gospel (Isaiah 11:2);*
- *be a prophet like Moses (Deuteronomy 18:15);*
- *be a light to the nations offering salvation to all (Isaiah 42:6–7);*
- *enter Jerusalem humbly, riding on a donkey (Zechariah 9:9);*
- *be forsaken by God the Father while bearing the sins of humanity (Psalm 22:1; Isaiah 53:3–6, 10–12);*

- *be mocked at his crucifixion (Psalm 22:6);*
- *suffer from pierced limbs and thirst as men gambled for his clothes (Psalm 22:16–18);*
- *suffer, be rejected, be killed, and be assigned a burial with the wicked (Isaiah 53: 3–9);*
- *be raised from the dead on the third day (Hosea 6:2).*[43]

This sampling of prophecies regarding Christ from the Old Testament provides a glimpse into the connections between the Hebrew Scriptures and the New Testament Christ. In his Gospel, Luke even recounted one of Jesus' post-resurrection appearances where Jesus traveled with two of his followers "and beginning with Moses and all the prophets he carefully unveiled to them the revelation of himself throughout the Scriptures" (Luke 24:27). The Scriptures mentioned here are those of the Old Testament—the only written words of God that the Jews had available to them during Jesus' lifetime.

Jesus and the Scriptures (Old Testament *and* New Testament) are so interconnected that Christian theologian Norman Geisler can write, "Christ is the key to the interpretation of the Bible, not only in that He is the fulfillment of Old Testament types and prophecies, but in that Christ is the thematic unity of the whole span of scriptural revelation."[44] Jesus, God's Son, is the key to the Bible, God's Word. The living Word (Jesus Christ) is woven throughout the written Word (the Bible).

So, according to the apostle Peter, who verifies the Scriptures? Jesus does. Who authenticates that Jesus is the Son of God? God the Father does. And who saw Jesus' resplendent divine glory? Peter (along with James and John) did.

The Divine Word's Impact

- *What did Peter say that students of Scripture would discover about Scripture if they remain "focused on it" (2 Peter 1:19; also see TPT footnotes 'd'–'h')?*

- *What has been the impact of your study and use of the Bible? How has it influenced your thinking, your behavior, and your relationships with other people?*

Facts about Prophecy

Peter discussed "prophecy"—by which he meant here the written word of God—in verses 20–21, and he mentioned three facts about it.

1. Scripture's interpretation requires the involvement of the Holy Spirit (v. 20).

2. Scripture "does not originate from someone's own imagination" (v. 20) or "initiative" (v. 21).

3. Scripture is "inspired by the moving of the Holy Spirit upon those who spoke the message that came from God" (v. 21).

- *What do these facts tell you about the source of Scripture? From where does it come?*

- *What do these facts tell you about what or who is needed to properly understand Scripture?*

- *What do these facts tell you about where Scripture does not originate?*

So while the books of the Bible have human authors, what they wrote is what God wanted them to write.[45] The Bible's words are God's words. And since they come from God, we can trust them.

EXPERIENCE GOD'S HEART

God's heart is for you to trust his written Word, to see it as coming from him for you—in fact, for all of us who trust him and seek to serve him.

- *Do you trust God's written word as inspired by him? Why or why not?*

- *Do you see and encounter Jesus in your reading and studying of God's Word? Why or why not?*

- *Turn to Jesus' prayer for his disciples in John 17. As you read it, reflect on what Jesus asks of the Father and how it relates to you. Thank him for how his prayer requests have been realized in your life. And praise him for what this prayer reveals about who Jesus is and how much he loves you.*

SHARE GOD'S HEART

- *Regardless of whether you know the Bible inside and out or often seem to need to look up that Bible verse you can't quite remember, why do you think it's important to know the Bible well? How does your knowledge of God impact your ability to share Jesus with others?*

- *Think about an experience that you had with God that really impacted your life. Then, like Peter did (2 Peter 1:16–18), share that experience with someone, using it in a way that will help that person better rest in the reliability of God's Word and/or the reality of Jesus as God's Son.*

Talking It Out

1. What's one big takeaway you have from your study of 2 Peter 1:12–21? How does your answer connect with one of the main themes of this letter?

2. Truth matters, as does the evidence we have to support it. What are some truths of the Christian faith that you firmly believe, and why do you believe them? What evidential support can you provide for them?

3. What are some truths that you want to pass along to others and urge them to remember before you leave this earth? Why do these truths matter so much to you?

LESSON 9

False Teachers

(2 Peter 2)

In a fallen world, truth has its enemies. Even the ancient Hebrews had to face that fact. Before they entered the promised land, they wondered, "'How will we know whether or not a prophecy is from the LORD?'" (Deuteronomy 18:21 NLT). Here's the test for authenticity God gave them: "If the prophet speaks in the LORD's name but his prediction does not happen or come true, you will know that the LORD did not give that message. That prophet has spoken without my authority and need not be feared" (v. 22 NLT). But what if a prophet performs signs and miracles and then urges people to follow foreign gods? Should that prophet be considered a true prophet? To that query Moses told the Hebrews, "Do not listen" to such prophets, for "God is testing you to see if you truly love him with all your heart and soul" (13:3 NLT).

During Jesus' ministry, he added another way to tell false prophets from true ones. He said that they will appear benign but inwardly "they are…ravenous wolves" (Matthew 7:15). And how will their true intentions become known? "You can spot them by their actions" (v. 16). Their true character will be revealed through what they do.

To these tests the apostle John added another. Just after urging Christians to "examine" "every spirit" so that they can "determine if they are of God" (1 John 4:1), he provided a "test for those with the genuine Spirit of God: they will confess Jesus as the Christ who has come in the flesh" (v. 2). Those individuals or groups motivated by false spirits will refuse to "acknowledge that Jesus is from God" (v. 3). These have "the spirit of antichrist" (v. 3).

From what these passages tell us, we can tell when anti-Christian error is afoot when (1) a prophecy allegedly from God fails to occur, (2) a so-called spokesperson of God tries to draw us away from the true God and toward false gods, (3) the person's actions reveal a character not attuned to divine sanctioned morality, and/or (4) a person or group will not accept that Jesus came in the flesh from the true God.

In 2 Peter 2, the apostle Peter zeroed in on false teachers, their activities, their teachings, and the outcomes of their ways. In the process, he helped us learn how to identify them and explained why we should refuse to follow them.

- *Before digging into the details of 2 Peter 2, read through the entire chapter to gain an overview of what Peter said. What would you say was his main point in this chapter?*

Characteristics of False Teachers

Peter began his warning about false teachers by first pointing out that they are like the "false prophets" that worked among God's people during Israel's history (2 Peter 2:1). Then he turned his attention to "false teachers" who will continue to spread untruth among followers of Christ (v. 1).

- *How will false teachers get inside our gatherings (v. 1)?*

- *What will these false teachers seek to do, and what will they bring with them (v. 1 and TPT footnote 'e')?*

From this point through the end of chapter 2, Peter never said what these false teachers will teach. The closest he came was saying that they will promise freedom (v. 19)—a freedom that is truly just slavery to corruption. Perhaps it's best that he didn't tell us what the positive content of their teaching will be, for false teachers have abounded in church history, and their teaching has varied considerably. What Peter did say, however, is what false teachers will deny, impugn, slander, despise, insult, and seek to destroy—all the while showing what their true obsessions are.

- *Who will false teachers deny and despise (vv. 1, 10)?*

- *Who, then, will they accept as authorities in their lives (v. 3)?*

- *False teachers "are willfully arrogant and insolent" (v. 10). How could false teachers demonstrate willful arrogance and/or insolence in the manner in which they live their lives or teach or preach?*

- *What are false teachers actually committed to (vv. 2–3, 13–15, 18–19)?*

- *What or who do they put down or exploit so they can exalt themselves and get what they want (vv. 2–3, 12, 14)?*

- *What will false teachers eventually receive for their efforts (vv. 1, 3, 12–13, 17, 19)?*

- *Who are false teachers and their fate compared to (vv. 4–10, 12, 15–17)?*

- *From these comparisons, what picture(s) forms in your mind about false teachers?*

- *How will false teachers affect "the way of truth" (v. 2)?*

- *Read Matthew 7:15–23. How does this passage relate to Peter's description of a false teacher in 2 Peter 2:2?*

- *Review your answers in this section. How would you now describe a false teacher?*

THE EXTRA MILE

Peter mentioned by way of example the non-Israelite prophet Balaam when discussing "prophets who love profit" (vv. 15–16). The Old Testament has Balaam's story recorded in Numbers 22–24, and the author of Jude also mentions Balaam in verse 11.

Peter's brief description of Balaam is this: "Balaam, son of Beor, who was rebuked for evil by a donkey incapable of speech yet that spoke with a human voice and restrained the prophet's madness" (2 Peter 2:15–16). Here are the central details.

As the full story of Balaam unfolds, Balaam (known in the region east of the promised land as a diviner and for his particular ability to bless and curse effectively) was tasked by Balak, the king of Moab, to curse the Israelites. Balak was afraid of them after hearing how they destroyed the Amorites. God told Balaam he couldn't follow through with the request, because the Israelites were blessed and belonged to Yahweh. So Balaam refused to go, telling Balak he could only speak what God told him.

After receiving a second message from Balak (and the promise of great honor and wealth), Balaam decided to go with him. On the way, Balaam's donkey saw the angel of the Lord blocking their path and refused to move. After Balaam struck the stubborn donkey three times, the donkey miraculously spoke and rebuked him. God opened Balaam's eyes, revealing the angel and admonishing Balaam. Balaam then met up with Balak and ended up blessing the Israelites three times. Balak was obviously frustrated by the entire experience, but Balaam was entirely restricted to the words that God gave him to speak. Balaam ended up prophesying God's favor and the future glory of Israel.

- *If you read the story of Balaam carefully, you'll notice that God gave Balaam permission to go to Balak (Numbers 22:20), but at the same time, "God's anger was kindled because he went" (v. 22 ESV). Why was God angry with Balaam? What do you ascertain as Balaam's true intent upon receiving permission from God to go to Balak?*

- *What can you infer about the relationship between greed and prophecy after considering the story of Balaam in Numbers 22–24 and Peter's mention of Balaam in 2 Peter 2? Reflect on how both texts address the issue of greed and its influence. How can you use the example of Balaam to help you in your assessment of potential false teachers and false teaching?*

The Choice to Choose Error

Peter had a good deal to say about false teachers, including what they are like, what they demean, and the judgment they will incur. He ended chapter 2 of his letter with a description of how many false teachers become what they are. He explained it this way: before any of us come to Christ, we are caught in our sin and thereby separated from God. This is as true of false teachers as it is of true ones. Some false teachers will never even desire to know Christ; they are cons through and through. Others, however, before they become false teachers, will attempt to "escape the corrupting forces of this world system through the experience of knowing about our Lord and Savior, Jesus the Messiah" (v. 20). The key here is "knowing about." They may come to know who Jesus is, what he did on the cross, and why. They may learn more about the history and teachings of the Christian faith. They may even join a Bible study and attend church for a season. But their "belief that" never really turns into a "belief in." They never fully give themselves by faith into the hands of the living God. Genuine confession and repentance, full trust in the Savior and Lord—such things never occur and are not truly present in their lives. While believing *that* some Christian teachings are true, they never actually believe *in* those truths. There is a big difference between accepting certain Christian teachings as true or "factual" and entrusting oneself fully to those truths, including to the One who is the fullness of truth (John 14:6; 1:14, 17; Colossians 2:3).

- *So what eventually happens to such people? What do they finally choose for their lives (2 Peter 2:20)?*

- *What is Peter's assessment of their eventual life choice (v. 21)?*

- *What do such individuals demonstrate about themselves (v. 22)?*

- *Can you see how people like this could become false teachers? Why or why not?*

- *Have you known anyone like who Peter described in verses 20–22? Tell a bit about this person.*

EXPERIENCE GOD'S HEART

- *God's heart is for his children to pursue holiness and righteousness. Given this, why is it so important for you to recognize the signs of false teachers, their lifestyles, and their motivations?*

- *God delivered Noah and Lot (vv. 5–8). How does their deliverance relate to the overall message of this chapter? How does the reality of their deliverance serve as an encouragement to you (v. 9)?*

SHARE GOD'S HEART

- *How does this chapter highlight the importance of both discernment and the pursuit of truth in your life? In your interactions with loved ones, especially those who may be following false teachers or teachings, how can you communicate these aspects of God's heart?*

- *Consider how you might confront false teachers and false teachings, whether you are confronting the source or those following the source. How can you do this in a way that both addresses the issue but also reflects God's desire for his truth to be spoken and taught?*

Talking It Out

1. Consider how Peter described false teachers. What do you see as their overall motivation, if you had to summarize it with a few words or a phrase? Given your answer, are there any authors, preachers, or teachers that you follow that you should consider no longer following?

2. Have you ever encountered a false teacher or false teaching? How did you handle the situation? What, if anything, would you now do differently?

3. Do you think that your study of 2 Peter has improved your discernment when it comes to detecting false teachers or teachings? Why or why not?

LESSON 10

Mockers and Last-Days Christians

(2 Peter 3)

Like his first letter, Peter's "second letter" to his readers was part of the overall purpose he had "to stir you up and awaken you to a proper mind-set" (3:1). Peter wanted his readers to think clearly, truly, and accurately about a number of matters, including the nature of God, the nature of salvation, life in God's forever family, suffering and persecution, the origin and inspiration of Scripture, and false teachers. The last chapter of his second letter will add yet another matter that he wants his readers to grasp: how to live as last-days Christians. What he told them has even more relevance to us in our day, for we are two thousand years closer to the events he described as yet to come.

The Matter at Hand

In 3:3, Peter identified the problem he wanted his readers to understand. The problem would be the multiplication of "mockers" who would be "chasing after their evil desires" and challenging Christian truths (vv. 3–4). These mockers are the false teachers Peter already described and critiqued in chapter 2. Their number will grow; their denials of truth will become more boisterous, slanderous, irrational, deceptive, and cunning; and their lives will be marked by immorality.

- *In 2 Peter 3, the apostle told us about one of the challenges mockers will create. What is it (v. 4)?*

- *It's fair to say that the mockers know that Christians are waiting for Jesus expectantly and eagerly. These Christians are their target audience. What emotions might mockers play on as they insult Christians who are waiting for Jesus' return?*

- *Peter answers the mockers' challenge to Jesus' second coming (vv. 5–10). Let's walk through his answer by answering the questions that follow:*

  What have these mockers overlooked (v. 5)?

  During the creation process of the entire universe, how did God bring about dry land and oceans on earth (v. 5)?

How did God later use water to impact earth's dry land (v. 6)?

All of these events demonstrate the awesome power of God, what he can do by just his word. They also show that God has no problem intervening into his creation when and how he wishes. Note also the implied time difference between the initial creation of the universe and the Noahic flood. These events show that God is not limited by time. His power remains the same no matter how much time passes by. Given all of this, God will use his power to do what to the ungodly (v. 7)?

What is time to God (v. 8)?

What does God's relationship to time mean for us when we consider God delivering on his promises (v. 9)? Is the supposed delay of Jesus' second coming a sign that it's not going to happen or that something else matters even more to God?

Will "the day of the Lord" come when we expect it to (v. 10)?

What will happen when the Lord returns (v. 10)?

- *Return now to the challenge that was posed by the mockers in verse 4. Basically, they were saying, "Jesus isn't coming back as he said he would. Our reason for saying this is that nothing has changed on earth. Our ancestors still die, and we still bury them." How does Peter's answer refute the mockers' challenge?*

- *Did you notice that there is a warning to the ungodly embedded in Peter's answer (v. 7) and a way of escape for them as well (v. 9)? What is the warning, and what is the way to avoid succumbing to what Peter warns against?*

How to Live as Last-Days Christians

Throughout the last chapter of 2 Peter, the apostle urged Jesus' followers to do certain things, to take certain actions. Faith is to be active, not passive. If we trust someone—have faith in them—then we should show it. This is especially so when it comes to our faith commitment to the triune Lord and what he reveals as the truth.

To see all that Peter wanted for and asked of his first-century readers—and, by extension, us—we'll need to go back over some ground that we have covered already in chapter 3. But now we are going to look at even that ground with a different focus.

- *Return to 3:1. What has Peter attempted to do so we can have something that he deems essential? And what is that essential thing, and why do you think it matters?*

- *What is the next action Peter wanted his readers to take (v. 2; TPT footnote 'g')? What importance did Peter place on knowing God's Word?*

- *What else did Peter call on us to do (v. 3)? Why is this important?*

- *What is the next thing Peter urged his readers to do (v. 8)? Why did he deem this so important to understand (v. 9)?*

- *In verse 11, Peter challenged us to see something. What is it, and what kind of action should it lead to on our part (vv. 11–12)?*

- *As we wait for what is yet to come, what should we do (v. 13)?*

- *Drawing a conclusion from what he has said, Peter called on us to take two actions. What are they (vv. 14–15)?*

- *In the final verses, Peter added yet two more actions we should take. What are they (vv. 17–18)?*

Interlude

In the midst of Peter's exhortations, he brought up a fellow apostle, Paul. Peter knew Paul. He respected Paul, accepting him as a fellow believer (Acts 9:26–28).[46] The apostle Peter even welcomed Paul into his home when Paul came to Jerusalem (Galatians 1:18). The two apostles clashed at one point during Paul's ministry (2:11–14), but what Peter later said about Paul in 2 Peter 3:15–16 implies that the two men had long been reconciled. Peter clearly recognized Paul's wisdom and close relationship to God.

In 3:15–16, Peter brought up Paul as an apostolic authority who believed what Peter had expressed in his two letters. Peter's evidence for this is Paul's own writings, which he conceded share "some concepts that are overwhelming to our understanding" (v. 16).

- *Go to the TPT footnote for verse 16. What explanation does it provide for Peter's comment?*

- *Have you ever found ideas taught in Scripture that are hard to grasp? If so, name one or two of them and the difficulty you have with them.*

- *What have you done to resolve the questions you have on these ideas?*

- *Peter added how some people use hard-to-understand ideas to do what (v. 16)?*

- *What does that tell you about the importance of regularly studying God's Word?*

- *Finally, Peter fit Paul's writings into which category of writings (v. 16)?*

Praise

- *Peter ended his second letter with words of praise for "our Lord and Savior, Jesus Christ" (v. 18). What did he want Jesus to receive and for how long?*

EXPERIENCE GOD'S HEART

- *Peter ended his letter with praise. Take some time to praise "our Lord and Savior, Jesus Christ" (v. 18). He deserves your praise for who he is, what he has done, what he is doing in your life right now, and what he will do soon and into the unending future.*

God's heart for you is to live like a last-days Christian. This will leave you well-prepared mentally to deal with those who oppose the Christian lifestyle (like the mockers who Peter described in chapter 3), and well-prepared spiritually so that you will be able to stand firm in your faith regardless of your situation.

- *For each of the following characteristics, add your thoughts regarding any application needed for your own life.*

    Last-days Christians have pure minds.

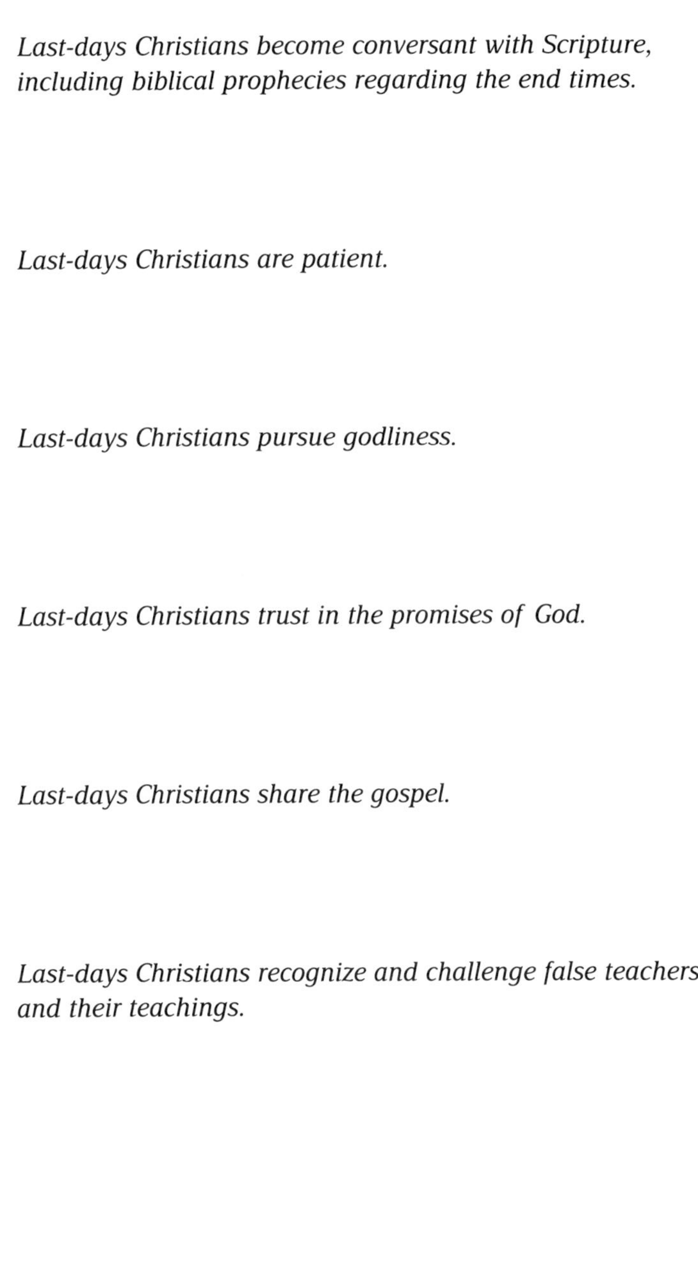

Last-days Christians become conversant with Scripture, including biblical prophecies regarding the end times.

Last-days Christians are patient.

Last-days Christians pursue godliness.

Last-days Christians trust in the promises of God.

Last-days Christians share the gospel.

Last-days Christians recognize and challenge false teachers and their teachings.

SHARE GOD'S HEART

- *Jesus will return. This was Jesus' promise. This is God's plan. How does the imminent return of Jesus shape your message of hope and salvation as you share the gospel with unbelievers and as you encourage your brothers and sisters in Christ, especially when they are facing trials?*

- *Jesus' return will involve salvation, but it will also involve judgment. How does this duality affect the way you share the love of God with others? How can you share the message of God's justice, along with his mercy, in a way that reflects his grace and love?*

- *Peter encouraged Christians to be "consumed with godliness" (v. 11) in anticipation and preparation for Jesus' return. How can you encourage others to pursue godliness in a way that reflects God's heart for his people and those who are lost?*

Talking It Out

1. Why is it so important for Christians to understand the Bible, including its prophecies, Jesus' commands, and the apostles' instructions?

2. When culture seems so against Christianity—and when mockers and skeptics flourish—what strategies do you use to maintain and defend your faith?

3. As a Christian, you already have the Holy Spirit at work inside you, and hopefully, that knowledge and experience encourages you to pursue godliness. How does the certain but unexpected second coming of Jesus also encourage your pursuit of godliness (3:10–12)?

4. In its introduction for each book, the TPT captures the central theme of 1 Peter as “triumphant hope” and the central theme of 2 Peter as “triumphant grace.” Discuss Peter’s two letters. If you were asked to state the main theme of each letter, what would you say and why?

LESSON 11

Jude: You *Can* Handle the Truth!

(Jude 1–13)

The last of the three New Testament letters in our study is Jude (or Judah, which is the name we will use in our study lessons). It has no chapters and contains just twenty-five verses, so it's short. The only New Testament letters shorter than Judah are 2 John, 3 John, and Philemon.

As we'll soon see, Judah's focus is a challenge to his readers. He wants them to "vigorously defend and contend for the beliefs that we cherish" (v. 3). In other words, Judah calls on his readers to fight for the truth!

If you have seen the movie *A Few Good Men*, you may recall the court scene where the defense attorney (played by Tom Cruise) of two marines questions Colonel Jessep (played by Jack Nicholson) who is testifying on the stand, pushing him to tell the truth of what he knows. The exchange between the two men becomes so intense that Colonel Jessep finally and angrily belts out, "You can't handle the truth!" This now-famous line was not the one written in the script. Nicholson was supposed to say, "You already have the truth!" But his improvised line is what came out and it became one of the most famous lines in movie history.[47]

As we approach the little letter of Judah, we find that Judah wanted his readers to defend the truth they already have and know. He believed they could handle the opposition against the truth, so he challenged them to do just that.

- *Before we delve into the details of this letter, take the time to read through it now. Then jot down here what stands out to you about what you find.*

Author and Date

This letter is named after its author. Judah is his Hebrew name, and Jude or Judas is his name in Greek.

- *In verse 1, how did the author introduce himself?*

Notice that Judah referred to himself as a "brother of Jacob" (v. 1). This Jacob has a New Testament book named after him, at least in the Greek. You see, the book normally referred to as James in the New Testament should be called Jacob, for "there is no 'James' in Greek; it is Jacob."[48] This man Jacob was a brother to Judah, and both men were brothers of Jesus. In two places in the Gospels, Jacob and Judah are both mentioned as brothers of Jesus (Matthew 13:55; Mark 6:3). However, neither Jacob nor Judah believed that their brother Jesus was the long-awaited Savior (John 7:5)—not until, that is, he rose from the dead and demonstrated that he was alive (1 Corinthians 15:5, 7). It was only then that they were counted among the 120 believers who were praying together in Jerusalem before the coming of the Holy Spirit (Acts 1:13–15).

Now, Jacob eventually became the presiding leader of the Jerusalem church, and he also received the title of apostle, even though he was not one of the original Twelve (Acts 12:17; 15:13; 21:18; Galatians 1:18–19; 2:9). Ancient church historian Eusebius (ca. 265–339) told us that Jacob was even surnamed "the Just" due to his eminent virtue.[49]

Concerning Judah, on the other hand, all we know about him is what has already been mentioned. He was not an apostle, and he was not well-known in the early church. To identify himself, he mentioned his relationship to Jacob, who many Christians would have known. And although he was one of Jesus' brothers, he doesn't lean on that relationship. Rather, he referred to himself as a "loving servant of Jesus"—a humble way to associate himself with the Lord.

While Judah was a bit obscure, his little letter was not. Many of the church fathers of the second, third, fourth, and fifth centuries mentioned his letter, quoted from it, or alluded to it. By the end of the second century, the churches in Rome, Africa, and Egypt had clearly accepted his letter as divine Scripture. While some Christians questioned the letter's use of two possible apocryphal books, this issue failed to keep the book out of the canon of Scripture.[50]

- *Judah knew Jesus as a child and grew up with him. He saw him start his ministry, perform miracles, preach, and teach, but Judah didn't initially believe that Jesus was the promised Messiah. Later, Judah believed and became an author of one of the books of the Bible. What is the significance of having a letter written by one of Jesus' brothers?*

- *With the exception of John, who died of natural causes around AD 95, all the apostles were martyred by the early seventies.*[51] *What is the significance of Judah not only mentioning the teachings of the apostles on several occasions in this short letter but also calling for the apostles' teachings to be remembered (v. 17)?*

Dating the book of Judah is fairly difficult. Some scholars think Judah wrote his letter in the late fifties, while others believe his letter may have been composed much later, perhaps between AD 65 and 80. Scholars present various arguments for each position, but none are definitive. In the TPT's introduction to this letter, the date provided for it is AD 58–60, but the footnotes for verses 3–4 show why it's possible that the letter was composed sometime after 2 Peter was. In other words, all we know for sure is that the author wrote Judah during the latter half of the first century.[52]

Audience

Similar to the difficulty in assigning a specific date to Judah, there is some difficulty in assigning a specific audience as well. However, given the general time period during which Judah was likely written and given the connections between Judah and 2 Peter, it's likely that Judah was addressing early Christians in the eastern Mediterranean area, perhaps in Asia Minor or Syrian Antioch.[53]

Purpose and Major Themes

Judah himself explained that his initial intent was to write in celebration of "our amazing salvation we all participate in" (v. 3). However, he felt compelled to change his focus from salvation to apologetics, from the gospel to the defense of the Christian faith. Though only a short twenty-five verses in length, Judah is filled with urgent warnings and relevant commands for Christians when they find themselves needing to defend their beliefs.

In Judah's time, the reason for his emphasis on fighting for the faith was due to a terrible infiltration problem in the churches under his care.

- *Read Judah 4. What had occurred that provoked Judah's concern?*

- *What truth of Christianity was being perverted by individuals who were using the Christian teaching about grace to justify immorality and to turn away from Jesus Christ?*

There are four themes that Judah addressed.

1. Defense of the faith. Judah related the need for sound doctrine as Christians shared the gospel and presented the fullness of Christian truth. As you read this letter, you'll be moved to go beyond defending a simple belief in God to contending for truth in all aspects of the Christian faith.

- *Recall a time you've had to defend not only your belief in God but your Christian faith in general. What was that experience like?*

- *What did you use as your evidence to back up your beliefs?*

2. Live the faith. Judah was concerned with not only the basis of the Christian faith but also with how followers of Jesus live out their faith.

- *This letter contains several recommendations for the proper manner in which a Christian should live out their faith, which will be specifically addressed in Lesson 12. What are some ways in which you live out your faith? Write them down here so you can compare them with what Judah said toward the end of his letter.*

- *How does living out your faith help you to preserve and deepen your faith?*

3. The character of God. There are many aspects of God revealed in Judah. For example, similar to 1 and 2 Peter, Judah reveals God's triune nature. The author of Judah also characterized God as protector and savior.

- *What are some of your favorite characteristics of God?*

- *What characteristics of God has God revealed to you, and how has he revealed them?*

4. The coming salvation and judgment. Jesus' return must have always been on the minds of the early Christians, especially those who met with him after his resurrection and, even more so, for those who saw his ascension and heard him speak of his return. Judah spoke to the fullness of salvation that will come with Jesus' second coming, and he added to that the judgment that the ungodly can expect upon the Lord's return.

- *Judah connected salvation and judgment. What relationship do you see between these two events?*

The Stories Behind the Stories

Judah made it clear that various individuals who had snuck into Christian gatherings were advancing licentiousness and a denial of Jesus' lordship, trying to get Christians to adhere to their false teaching and immoral lifestyle. To impress upon believers how serious this threat was, Judah brought up several stories, most of which he pulled from the Old Testament, to demonstrate the judgment God brings upon recalcitrant unbelievers.

One of Judah's stories comes from a Jewish pseudepigraphal book called 1 Enoch. Jewish pseudepigraphal books were written between 200 BC and AD 200. Christian scholars Norman Geisler and William Nix described these as "false and spurious writings" that "represent the religious lore of the Hebrews in the intertestamental period."[54] While neither Jews nor Christians accepted them as Scripture, many Jews and Christians read them.

Returning to Judah, verse 14 cites words preserved in 1 Enoch 1:9 almost verbatim, and verse 15 of Judah more loosely restates what chapter 1, verse 10 of 1 Enoch says. Judah's use of this story does not imply that he regards the book of 1 Enoch to be on par with inspired Scripture. It does show, however, that Judah believed that his initial readers would be familiar with that book and have a certain degree of respect for it. (The apostle Paul followed a similar strategy in Acts 17:28, when he spoke to an audience of pagan philosophers in Athens. There, Paul also cited pagan writers in his defense of the gospel, using writers his audience would know and respect.) In Judah's case, he recognized that "what Enoch had said…turned out to be a true prophecy in view of the ungodly conduct of these false teachers."[55]

The other book outside of the Old Testament that Judah apparently refers to is the Assumption of Moses. Three early church fathers—Clement of Alexandria (ca. 155–220), Origen (ca. 185–254), and Didymus (ca. 309–398)—believed that Judah used this book in verse 9. But we cannot double-check the veracity of this belief because the Assumption of Moses did not survive; we have no copies of it, just three quotes from it. So while it's possible that Judah cited from it, he may also have been referring to a traditional story that could have been the basis of the longer work called the Assumption of Moses. We just don't know for sure.[56] Regardless, Judah referred to a story about Moses that his readers must have known, and he used it to make a point of refutation against the immorality and false teaching of the individuals who were striving to turn Christians away from the Lord and the truth.

Let's take a closer look at the stories Judah used.

- *For each story listed, read the applicable Bible verses and then write out the following: (1) a brief summary of the story; (2) how Judah uses it to advance his argument; and (3) how it can serve as a warning and/or encouragement to you.*

    1) The Hebrews' exodus from Egypt (Judah 5; Exodus 12:23–41; 14:1–31)

    2) Rebellious fallen angels before the Noahic flood (Judah 6 and TPT footnote 'e'; Genesis 6:1–8; 2 Peter 2:4–5)

    3) Sodom and Gomorrah (Judah 7; Genesis 18:20—19:29; 2 Peter 2:6–8)

    4) The archangel Michael and Moses' body (Judah 8–9 and TPT footnotes for these verses)

    5) Cain (Judah 11; Genesis 4:1–15)

6) Balaam (Judah 11 and TPT footnote 'j'; Numbers 22–24; 2 Peter 2:15–16[57])

7) Korah (Judah 11 and TPT footnote 'k'; Numbers 16:1–40)

- *According to all of these illustrious examples, what is the fate of the ungodly?*

- *Since that is their fate, why would any Christian want to follow them instead of Jesus Christ?*

- *Should such ungodly individuals be envied or pitied, respected or shunned, allowed to further permeate Christian gatherings or cast out of them? What do you think? Consider how God dealt with them as you ponder this question.*

How to Spot an Apostate: Part 1

Like Peter in his letters, Judah placed a heavy focus on a Christian's ability to be able to recognize false teachers and their teachings.

- *Complete the table below by (1) reading the accompanying verse from Judah, (2) checking out the characteristic, and (3) adding an example or thought of your own. As you complete the chart, for example, you might realize your own tendency to exhibit one of the characteristics listed; if so, how can you work to give that to God and replace it with a characteristic of God that is more reflective of your heart for Jesus? Another example could be a realization of a false teacher or teaching that has affected or is affecting your faith. (Part 2 of the chart is found in Lesson 12).*

False Teachers and Their Teaching, Part 1

Verse from Judah	Characteristic	Added Example or Thought
4	Is depraved	
4	Is immoral	
4	Denies Christ	
8	Is corrupt	
8	Rejects authority	
8	Blasphemes/lacks respect for the spiritual realm	
8	Mocks	
10	Is ignorant	
10	Is irrational	
10	Is self-destructive	
11	Is greedy	

EXPERIENCE GOD'S HEART

- *Jude contains several warnings, by way of direct statements and examples, about false teachers and false teachings. Reflect on how God values integrity and truth in the church. How can you be more vigilant in guarding against potential deception that could present itself among your family, friends, and church family and thereby negatively affect their faith?*

- *Consider God's desire for you to live in holiness and how that desire for you stands in direct contrast to the wishes of false teachers. Overall, what do you see as God's heart for you as you strive to remain holy, especially in the face of potential apostates or false teachers?*

- *What has Jude 1–13 revealed to you about how God responds to those who pervert his people and his ways? God is committed to justice. How has he demonstrated this commitment in your life?*

SHARE GOD'S HEART

- *To effectively confront error, we must know the truth and why it is true. But it takes time to learn even the basic teachings of the Christian faith and why we should accept them as true. It also takes time to learn how to study God's Word and gain enough of a handle on it that we can explain, apply, and defend it. So you can better share God's heart with others, consider what you can do to improve your understanding of Christian teaching and the Bible. Bible studies such as this one will help you work through Scripture. For more help in understanding the Bible and Christian teaching, check out the resources mentioned in the endnote at the end of this sentence.*[58] *Just remember, you are learning, not just for yourself but also for those you can help.*

- *How can you use what Judah says about the just end of the ungodly to better communicate what Jesus' death and resurrection are meant to save human beings from? In other words, how can you use the bad news about the fate of human beings to convey the good news about how we can be delivered from that awful end? Ask the Lord to show you when you can share this good news/bad news situation with someone who needs to hear it.*

Talking It Out

1. Judah was Jesus' brother. Reflect on how his initial intent in writing his letter was to talk about "our amazing salvation" (Judah 3). Why was salvation so amazing for Judah? What could it have to do with being Jesus' brother?

2. Judah 12–13 describes false teachers with several metaphors: "dangerous hidden reefs," "clouds with no rain," "fruitless late-autumn trees," "wild waves of the sea," and "wandering stars." Choose a few of these metaphors and discuss how they reflect the true nature of an ungodly false teacher.

3. Judah 12 mentions Christian "love feasts." What did a "love feast" look like in the early Christian church? (See TPT footnote 'l' for this verse, as well as Acts 2:42–47 and 1 Corinthians 11:17–34.)

LESSON 12

Perseverance

(Jude 14–25)

"History repeats itself" is a popular phrase in culture. But that quote is really a paraphrase of something George Santayana wrote. It actually comes from Santayana's book *Reason in Common Sense*. The actual quote goes like this: "Those who cannot remember the past are condemned to repeat it." That's a great thought to consider as you come to the end of your study of Judah. Judah drew from history to remind his readers of the fate of the ungodly, giving Christians ample reason to avoid falling prey to the then most recent manifestation of ungodliness—licentiousness and the denial of Jesus Christ as Lord.

In a fallen world, sin abounds and will continue until our Lord puts an end to it and ushers in a new world, forever free of corruption (Revelation 20–22). Until then, our ultimate enemy "roams around incessantly, like a roaring lion looking for its prey to devour" (1 Peter 5:8). We need to remain on guard, holding firm to the truth, especially the truths of our Christian faith. Otherwise, we are in danger of repeating the worst side of history, falling prey again and again to the forces arrayed against God—forces who will meet a final end of divine judgment.

Enoch Was Right

As we pointed out in the last lesson, Judah referred to the Jewish pseudepigraphal book of 1 Enoch in verses 14–15. He did not claim that his use of 1 Enoch demonstrates that the book is inspired by God, but he did assert that something 1 Enoch says is actually true.

- *What truth did Judah cite from this non-biblical book (vv. 14–15)?*

- *Do Enoch's words support what Judah has argued so far? Support your answer.*

- *Why do you imagine that Judah used 1 Enoch rather than a biblical book?*

Is truth truth no matter where it comes from? Scripture suggests that it is. For instance, in the Old Testament, truth comes from a heathen diviner (Numbers 24:17) and even through a donkey (22:28). In the New Testament, the apostle Paul quoted from pagan poets, such as Aratus (Acts 17:28), Menander (1 Corinthians 15:33), and Epimenides (Titus 1:12).[59] Scripture is clear that the ultimate source of all truth is God who is truth (John 1:14; 14:6; 15:26; Romans 3:3–4). So when we come across truth in other writings, speeches, blogs, and so on, we can rest assured that it will not contradict him who is truth. And if it does, then it is not true!

- *Do you think that all truth is God's truth? Why or why not?*

How to Spot an Apostate: Part 2

Judah further described the characteristics of false teachers in verses 14–19.

- *Complete the chart below, continuing your work from the previous lesson. As a reminder, read the verse, read the word or phrase, and then add your own thoughts about it or another example.*

False Teachers and Their Teaching, Part 2

Verse from Judah	Characteristic	Added Example or Thought
16	Complains	
16	Is discontent	
16	Is self-interested	
16	Is arrogant	
16	Is manipulative	
18	Has ungodly motivation	
19	Causes division	
19	Is focused on the things of the world	
19	Does not live according to the Holy Spirit	

The Seven Commands of Jude

The book of Judah ends with the author giving seven commands (vv. 17–23). These commands are meant to encourage you and strengthen you as you build up your faith; live in anticipation of the second coming of Jesus; and (potentially) face an onslaught of false teachers, false teachings, and general opposition to the Christian faith.

- *As you consider each of the seven commands, think about (1) to what extent they are currently evident in your life and (2) how you can better apply them in your life. Journal at least a few sentences for each. There is also an accompanying question for each to aid you in your thinking.*

    1) *Remember the "prophecies of the apostles" (v. 17).* *How well do you know what the apostles taught and predicted?*

    2) *Build up your spiritual life (v. 20).* *How do you currently (and daily) work to build your spiritual life (e.g., daily Bible study, starting your day with worship, etc.)?*

    3) *Pray in the Holy Spirit (v. 20).* *Evaluate your prayer life. Do you pray throughout the day, working to constantly pray?*

4) ***Fasten your hearts to God's love (v. 21).*** *Imagine that God's love for you is like Niagara Falls, constantly pouring down and over you. Imagine, too, that you have a bucket to catch that loving overflow. How is your bucket turned—to catch the most you can or the least?*

5) ***Receive mercy from Jesus (v. 21).*** *How often and readily do you confess your sins and seek Jesus' help?*

6) ***Show compassion to those who doubt (v. 22).*** *Do you consider yourself a compassionate person? How do you currently demonstrate compassion, especially to those struggling with their Christian faith?*

7) ***Be merciful to the lost and work to save them (v. 23).*** *What are you doing to spread the gospel, including to those individuals you see as hard cases?*

8) ***Never compromise with sin (v. 23).*** *How do you strive to keep yourself pure, with your eyes on Jesus and not on the world?*

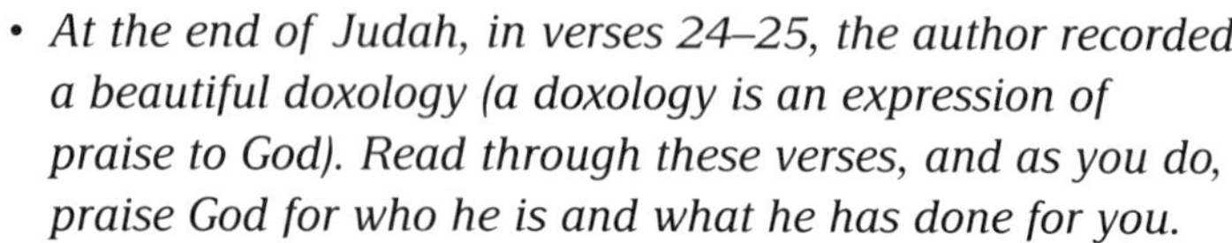

EXPERIENCE GOD'S HEART

- *At the end of Judah, in verses 24–25, the author recorded a beautiful doxology (a doxology is an expression of praise to God). Read through these verses, and as you do, praise God for who he is and what he has done for you.*

- *As a Christian, does God guarantee that you won't stumble? Have you stumbled lately?*

- *As a Christian, you are saved and guaranteed to have eternal life! But does that mean you are faultless? Why or why not?*

- *How do your answers to the two previous questions impact your view of God's heart for you, especially in the context of Judah's doxology?*

SHARE GOD'S HEART

When you share the love of Jesus with others, you show them the grace and mercy that God has for them. When you preach the gospel and when a person comes to believe in Jesus because of your efforts, Judah said that you literally "snatch others out of the fire to save them" (v. 23).

- *Why is it so important when sharing the love of Jesus with others that compassion and mercy take precedent?*

- *In Matthew 25:34–40, Jesus narrated the "Son of Man's" interactions with his people at the final judgment:*

> The King will turn to those on his right and say, "You have a special place in my Father's heart....For when you saw me hungry, you fed me. When you found me thirsty, you gave me drink. When I had no place to stay, you invited me in, and when I was poorly clothed, you covered me. When

> I was sick, you tenderly cared for me, and when I was in prison you visited me." Then the godly will answer him, "Lord, when did we see you hungry or thirsty and give you food and something to drink? When did we see you with no place to stay and invite you in? When did we see you poorly clothed and cover you? When did we see you sick and tenderly care for you, or in prison and visit you?" And the King will answer them, "Don't you know? When you cared for one of the least of these, my little ones, my true brothers and sisters, you demonstrated love for me."

- *How does Judah 22–23 speak to the heart of what Jesus said in this passage?*

- *When was the last time you reached out to someone who was really in need, whether their need was physical or spiritual? What did you learn about God's heart from that experience?*

Talking It Out

1. It's a great life skill to be able to summarize something you read or studied. With a few sentences, summarize the letter of Judah in your own words. Share your response with someone who isn't familiar with this letter. If writing isn't necessarily your thing, summarize the letter by telling someone else what it is about. Be brief, and at the same time see if you can convince someone who is unfamiliar with Judah to give it a read.

2. What does it look like for you when you contend for your faith (Judah 3)?

3. How does the book of Judah serve as a reminder to you that God has your back? What does God promise as you stand firm and work to "build yourselves up on the foundation of your most holy faith" (v. 20)?

4. If you had to choose one theme of 1 Peter, 2 Peter, and Judah that has had an impact on you, what would that theme be? Why?

5. Why were false teaching and immorality such concerns for Peter and Judah? Why might they still be concerns today?

6. If another Christian came to you seeking advice for how to stand firm in their faith, especially if they were feeling defeated in the face of opposition or if they were feeling stressed over being prepared for Jesus' return, what advice would you give them? Here's the catch: you can only give them one piece of advice, and it has to be something that both Peter and Judah would agree with.

Endnotes

1. Brian Simmons et al., "A Note to Readers," *The Passion Translation: The New Testament with Psalms, Proverbs, and Song of Songs* (Savage, MN: BroadStreet Publishing Group, 2020), ix.

2 See *The Passion Translation* (BroadStreet Publishing Group, 2020), footnotes for Matthew 16:18.

3 TPT, "1 Peter: Author and Audience."

4 In his book *New Testament Introduction*, 4th ed. (InterVarsity Press, 1990), Bible scholar Donald Guthrie examines the arguments for and against Peter's authorship of the letter that bears his name and finds that the evidence for his authorship is "more reasonable than any alternative hypothesis" (p. 781).

5 C. Suetonius Tranquillus, *The Lives of the Twelve Caesars*, 38, n.d., https://penelope.uchicago.edu.

6 Cornelius Tacitus, *The Annals*, 15.38, 15.44, n.d., https://www.perseus.tufts.edu/hopper.

7 Paul L. Maier, *In the Fullness of Time: A Historian Looks at Christmas, Easter, and the Early Church*, revised ed. (HarperSanFrancisco, 1991), 332–35.

8 J. R. Michaels, "1 Peter," *Dictionary of the Later New Testament and Its Developments*, eds. Ralph P. Martin and Peter H. Davids (InterVarsity Press, 1997), 919.

9 According to Christian tradition, Peter was crucified upside down in Rome on the orders of Nero in AD 69. See Thieleman J. van Braght, *Martyrs Mirror of the Defenseless Christians*, trans. Joseph F. Sohm (Herald Press, 1938), 79–81.

10 James Strong, "6918," *The New Strong's Expanded Dictionary of Bible Words* (Thomas Nelson, 2001), 777–778.

11 Strong, "40," *The New Strong's Expanded Dictionary of Bible Words*, 908–909.

12 Strong, "3610," *The New Strong's Expanded Dictionary of Bible Words*, 1261.

13 Lesley Adkins and Roy A. Adkins, *Handbook to Life in Ancient Rome* (Oxford University Press, 1994), 341; Michael Grant, *A Social History of Greece and Rome* (Charles Scribner's Sons, 1992), 102.

14 William L. Westermann, *The Slave Systems of Greek and Roman Antiquity* (The American Philosophical Society, 1955), chap. XIII.

15 A. A. Rupprecht, "Slave, Slavery," *Dictionary of Paul and His Letters*, eds. Gerald F. Hawthorne and Ralph P. Martin (InterVarsity Press, 1993), 881.

16 Rupprecht, "Slave, Slavery," 881.

17 "Slavery in Ancient Rome," The British Museum, n.d., https://www.britishmuseum.org.

18 Rupprecht, "Slave, Slavery," 881.

19 You can read more about the Simmons' story in the archived *Sports Illustrated* article, by S. L. Price, July 6, 1998, https://vault.si.com.

20 John Piper, "The Beautiful Faith of Fearless Submission," sermon, *Desiring God*, April 15, 2007, https://www.desiringgod.org.

21 Tim Challies, "Why We Cringe at 'Submit,'" *Challies*, April 30, 2018, https://www.challies.com.

22 Mary J. Evans, *Woman in the Bible* (InterVarsity Press, 1983), 117, emphasis added.

23 James Rochford, "(1 Peter 3:3) Does This Mean That Women Should Not Wear Makeup and Jewelry?" *Evidence Unseen*, 2024, https://www.evidenceunseen.com.

24 Aristotle, *Oeconomica*, 1.3.4., n.d., https://www.loebclassics.com.

25 Karen H. Jobes, *1 Peter*, Baker Exegetical Commentary on the New Testament series (Baker Academic, 2005), 209.

26 Jobes, *1 Peter*, 209.

27 Donald Miller, *Blue Like Jazz: Nonreligious Thoughts on Christian Spirituality* (Thomas Nelson, 2003), 34–35.

28 Fritz Rienecker, *A Linguistic Key to the Greek New Testament*, rev. ed., trans. and ed. by Cleon L. Rogers Jr. (Zondervan, 1980), 758.

29 Presenting the Christian faith clearly and persuasively takes preparation. Part of the preparation includes learning what the evidences are for the faith. Another is learning how to present those evidences. Here are some resources that will help you in both of these tasks. First, some online resources: *Reasonable Faith* podcast with William Lane Craig; *I Don't Have Enough Faith to Be an Atheist* podcast with Frank Turek; *Apologetics 315* podcast, Defenders Media. Now some printed resources: Gregory Koukl, *Tactics: A Game Plan for Discussing Your Christian Convictions*, 10th anniversary ed. (Zondervan, 2019); Norman L. Geisler and Paul K. Hoffman, eds., *Why I Am a Christian: Leading Thinkers Explain Why They Believe*, 2nd ed. (Baker Books, 2006); Kenneth Richard Samples, *Without a Doubt: Answering the 20 Toughest Faith Questions* (Baker Books, 2004); Lee Strobel, *The Case for Faith: A Journalist Investigates the Toughest Objections to Christianity*, updated ed. (Zondervan, 2021).

30 For more information about these spirits, which were fallen angels, or demons, see TPT, Genesis 6:1–4, footnote 'e'; and the TPT Bible study guide *TPT The Book of Genesis—Part 1* (BroadStreet Publishing Group, 2022), gen. ed. Brian Simmons, 143–45.

31 You can watch Bradbury's full race on YouTube: "The Most Unexpected Gold Medal in History – Steven Bradbury." https://www.youtube.com.

32 Kevin Giles, *Patterns of Ministry Among the First Christians*, 2nd ed. (Cascade Books, 2017), 104.

33 Giles, *Patterns of Ministry Among the First Christians*, 102.

34 Giles, *Patterns of Ministry Among the First Christians*, 102.

35 D. J. Tidball, "Social Setting of Mission Churches," in *Dictionary of Paul and His Letters*, 884.

36 K. N. Giles, "Church Order, Government," in *Dictionary of the Later New Testament and Its Development*, 222.

37 C. G. Kruse, "Ministry," in *Dictionary of Paul and His Letters*, 604.

38 "Miletus," *The New Unger's Bible Dictionary*, by Merrill F. Unger, rev. ed. (Moody Press, 1988).

39 Giles, *Patterns of Ministry Among the First Christians*, 107.

40 See TPT, 2 Peter, "Introduction," for a very brief treatment of one of the questions about this letter's authorship. For fuller treatments of the questions surrounding this letter's authorship and authenticity, see Edwin A. Blum, "2 Peter: Introduction," in *The Expositor's Bible Commentary*, gen. ed. Frank E. Gaebelein (Zondervan, 1981), vol. 12, 257–61; and Guthrie, *New Testament Introduction*, 805–54.

41 To learn more about how the twenty-seven books of the New Testament were finally acknowledged as Scripture by the church, see Norman L. Geisler and William E. Nix, *A General Introduction to the Bible*, rev. ed. (Moody Press, 1986), ch. 16.

42 TPT, footnote 'b' on 2 Peter 1:19.

43 For a fuller list of the Bible's prophecies concerning Jesus Christ, see J. Barton Payne, *Encyclopedia of Biblical Prophecy* (Harper & Row, 1973), 665–670.

44 Norman L. Geisler, *To Understand the Bible Look for Jesus*, reprint ed. (Baker Book House, 1979), 7.

45 To learn more about divine inspiration, see *A General Introduction to the Bible*, by Geisler and Nix, part one; and René Pache, *The Inspiration and Authority of Scripture*, trans. Helen I. Needham (Moody Press, 1969).

46 Before and for a while after Paul's conversion to Christ, he was known by his Jewish name, Saul. Later he went by his Roman name, Paul. This occurred when his ministry focus expanded beyond Jews to gentiles. Luke notes the name change in Acts 13:9. See also F. F. Bruce, "Paul in Acts and Letters," in *Dictionary of Paul and His Letters*, 681; and Unger, "Paul," *The New Unger's Bible Dictionary*, 968, 978; TPT, Acts 13:9, footnote 'l.'

47 Grace Gavilanes, "'You Can't Handle the Truth': 10 Famous Movie Lines That Were Actually Improvised," *People*, August 3, 2017, https://people.com/movies/famous-movie-lines-improvised.

48 TPT, James (Jacob), "Introduction."

49 Merrill F. Unger, "James," *The New Unger's Bible Dictionary*.

50 To learn more about the history of Judah's letter becoming recognized as God's word, see Edwin A. Blum, "Jude," *The Expositor's Bible Commentary*, 383; and Guthrie, *New Testament Introduction*, 901–902.

51 A great resource for an in-depth look at Christian tradition as it relates to the death of the apostles is the following: van Braght, *Martyrs Mirror of the Defenseless Christians*. For a quick take on the martyrdom of the apostles, see C. Michael Patton, "The Deaths of the Apostles," *Grace Bible Church*, n.d., http://www.gbcsl.com.

52 For discussions about the dating of this short letter, see R. L. Webb, "Jude," in *Dictionary of the Later New Testament and Its Developments*, 617–18; and Guthrie, *New Testament Introduction*, 905–909.

53 See Guthrie, *New Testament Introduction*, 913–14; Blum, "Jude," *The Expositor's Bible Commentary*, 383–84.

54 Geisler and Nix, *A General Introduction to the Bible*, 262.

55 Guthrie, *New Testament Introduction*, 915.

56 For more on the Assumption of Moses and its possible use in Judah's letter, see Guthrie, *New Testament Introduction*, 916.

57 See Lesson 9, "The Extra Mile."

58 To gain some basic knowledge about the Bible, including how it came down to us, see Norman L. Geisler and William E. Nix, *From God to Us: How We Got Our Bible* (Moody Press, 2012); and Geisler, *To Understand the Bible Look for Jesus*. When it comes to learning the basic teaching of Christianity, see John R. W. Stott, *Basic Christianity*, fiftieth anniversary ed. (Wm. B. Eerdmans, 2008); and C. S. Lewis, *Mere Christianity* (Macmillan, 1952). Helpful resources providing evidence for the reliability of the Bible and the Christian worldview can be found in endnote 30 of this study guide. All of these resources will get you started, for the riches of Scripture and Christian teaching are unending.

59 On this matter of Paul referring to pagan writers, see F. F. Bruce, *The Defense of the Gospel in the New Testament*, revised ed. (Wm. B. Eerdmans, 1977), chap. 4.